WARRIOR • 146

GERMAN PIONIER 1939–45

Combat Engineer of the Wehrmacht

GORDON L ROTTMAN   ILLUSTRATED BY CARLOS CHAGAS

Series editor Marcus Cowper

First published in Great Britain in 2010 by Osprey Publishing
Midland House, West Way, Botley, Oxford OX2 0PH, UK
44-02 23rd St, Suite 219, Long Island City, NY 11101, USA
E-mail: info@ospreypublishing.com

A CIP catalog record for this book is available from the British Library

Print ISBN 978 1 84603 578 4
PDF e-book ISBN 978 1 84908 2 693

Editorial by Ilios Publishing Ltd, Oxford, UK (www.iliospublishing.com)
Page layout by: Mark Holt
Index by Margaret Vaudrey
Typeset in Sabon and Myriad Pro
Originated by PPS Grasmere Ltd, Leeds, UK
Printed in China through Worldprint Ltd

10 11 12 13 14 10 9 8 7 6 5 4 3 2 1

ACKNOWLEDGEMENTS

The author is indebted to Joe E. Kaufmann, Nik Cornish, and Concord
Publications for their kind assistance.

ARTIST'S NOTE

Readers may care to note that the original paintings from which the
color plates in this book were prepared are available for private sale.
All reproduction copyright whatsoever is retained by the Publishers.
All enquiries should be addressed to:

Carlos Chagas,,
Rua Jose Higino 343 apto.204 – Tijuca,
Rio de Janeiro,
RJ, 20510-411,
Brazil

The Publishers regret that they can enter into no correspondence upon
this matter.

THE WOODLAND TRUST

Osprey Publishing are supporting the Woodland Trust, the UK's leading
woodland conservation charity, by funding the dedication of trees.

EDITOR'S NOTE

Throughout this book, the ß character has been used in some German
words. It corresponds to 'ss' in English.

ABBREVIATIONS

HJ	Hitlerjugend (Hitler Youth)
NCO	non-commissioned officer (*Unteroffizier*)
RAD	Reichsarbeitsdienst (National Labour Service)
RM	*Reichsmark* (National mark)
T-mine	*Tellermine* (platter mine – anti-tank mine)
S-mine	*Schrapnellmine* (shrapnel mine – anti-personnel mine)

PIONIER RANKS

Heer	US army equivalent
Pionier	Private
Oberpionier	Private 1st Class
Gefreiter	—
Unteroffizier-Anwärter	—
Obergefreiter mit weniger als 6 Dienstjahren	—
Obergefreiter mit mehr als 6 Dienstjahren	—
Stabsgefreiter	—
Unteroffizier	Corporal
Unterfeldwebel	Sergeant
Feldwebel	Staff Sergeant
Oberfeldwebel	Technical Sergeant
Hauptfeldwebel (appointment)	First Sergeant
Stabsfeldwebel	Master Sergeant

FOR A CATALOG OF ALL BOOKS PUBLISHED BY OSPREY
MILITARY AND AVIATION PLEASE CONTACT:

Osprey Direct, c/o Random House Distribution Center,
400 Hahn Road, Westminster, MD 21157
Email: uscustomerservice@ospreypublishing.com

Osprey Direct, The Book Service Ltd, Distribution Centre,
Colchester Road, Frating Green, Colchester, Essex, CO7 7DW
E-mail: customerservice@ospreypublishing.com

www.ospreypublishing.com

CONTENTS

GERMAN PIONIER 1939–45

INTRODUCTION

The German Army of World War II collectively referred to its various engineer units as *Pioniere* (pioneers). This organization included *Pioniertruppen* (pioneer troops), *Bautruppen* (construction troops), *Eisenbahntruppen* (railway troops – who both built and operated railroads), and *Technische Truppen* (technical troops). The *Pionieretruppen* were what in the West would be called combat engineers. They were thought of as assault troops first and construction workers second. These units were known as the *schwarz Pioniere* (black pioneers) owing to the black arm of service colour worn on uniforms. This differentiated them from the *weiss Pioniere* (white pioneers), who were combat engineer platoons assigned to infantry regiments. They were also known as the *Mädchen für Alles* (maids for all work) owing to the wide variety of jobs they undertook (see *FUBAR: Soldier Slang of World War II*, Gordon Rottman, Osprey: Oxford, 2007 for more of the rich German slang).

The divisional pioneer battalion (*Divisions Pionier-Bataillon*) was the basic pioneer unit encountered in the front lines and was considered a key unit necessary to support combat operations. On the march it reduced artificial and natural obstacles and repaired bridges. In addition, it assisted in crossing

A motor column crossing a river on a pontoon bridge, in this case a Bruckengerät B some 50m long and capable of supporting as much as 20 tons. While not evident here, anti-aircraft guns were normally emplaced to protect bridge sites. The Bruckengerät B could use two-piece metal pontoons *(Halbpontons)* or large inflatable boats. (Pier Paolo Battistelli)

water obstacles with portable bridging, pontoon ferries, assault boats, and inflatable boats. In the attack they breached obstacles and supported the infantry as specialist assault troops when attacking fortified positions with demolitions, flame-throwers, and smoke. In the defence they constructed fortifications and shelters, erected obstacles, laid minefields, planted booby traps, cleared fields of fire, erected camouflage, and maintained supply routes. In retreat they planted mines and booby traps, erected hasty obstacles, and destroyed bridges.

It was not uncommon for pioneer battalions to be employed as ad hoc infantry, especially late in the war when divisions were forced to defend wider than normal frontages and manpower was short. They also secured exposed flanks and gaps between units. On the Eastern Front they often had to provide rear area security against partisans.

RECRUITMENT

After the takeover of the German government by the National Socialist German Workers' Party (National-Sozialistische Deutsches Arbeiterparti – NSDAP) in 1933, the youth of Germany was bombarded with propaganda exalting the armed forces, the honour of military service, and the promised glory of the new Germany. Germany was indeed reawakening, reinvigorating itself after years of economic and political chaos, and it was the Nazis who were doing it. Democracy and capitalism had failed; Germany would regain its honour. Germany was being militarized and service in the Wehrmacht (Defence Force) was an obligation and honour for every fit German male. In 1935 laws were enacted to greatly expand the previously suppressed armed forces. No nation of the era had such an effective pre-military training program.

The first exposure to military life for most boys was the Hitler Youth (Hitlerjugend – HJ), which had existed in different forms since 1922. It expanded in 1933, but was not made compulsory until 1936, for boys aged from ten to 18. At that time there were five million members, increasing to eight million in 1940. Units were organized on a local basis with regular meetings, weekend encampments, and summer training camps. Basic military skills were taught: drill, map reading, first aid, gas defence, military ranks, competitive dummy grenade throwing, and a steady diet of propaganda lectures and films. Much emphasis was placed on sports and outdoor living. Marksmanship was undertaken using 5.6mm (.22cal) Mauser carbines. The effect was highly motivating and created a class of military aged, physically fit, partially trained young men dedicated to the Nazi regime (see Osprey Warrior 102: *The Hitler Youth 1933–45*, Alan Dearn, Osprey: Oxford, 2006).

The next step in a young man's path to military service was the National Labour Service (Reichsarbeitsdienst – RAD). Established in 1933, in mid-1934 six months' mandatory service was required from men aged between 19 and 25, followed by two years in the Wehrmacht. They lived in camps scattered throughout Germany receiving basic military training, but mostly they worked on the Westwall (Siegfried Line) and other fortifications, land reclamation, drainage control, agricultural land clearing, road building, and more. This prepared future soldiers for barracks life, military discipline, and improved their physical fitness. Toward the war's end these *Arbeitsmanner* were being transferred directly into Heer (army) pioneer and other units without additional training.

Improvisation and ingenuity were characteristic of the *Pioniere*, even though their makeshift solutions could not always be fully appreciated by the men using them. This improvised footway, built using medium-sized inflatable boats, planks, and timber, enables the infantry to get across the river, but judging from the look of the machine gunner in the foreground something more stable would have been appreciated. (Pier Paolo Battistelli)

A completed corduroy road was often settled in by running a tank or other heavy vehicle down it before the 'ribbon-cutting ceremony'. The guide rails on the edges were a standard fixture. Beneath the surface logs are at least five stringer logs running the length of the road surface. Depending on the depth of the mud it might require several layers of cross-laid logs. Ideally a layer of sand, earth, or gravel would be laid on the surface for a smoother ride.
(Nik Cornish at Stavka)

At age 16 boys were required to register at their defence replacement service station (*Wehrersatzdienststelle*), the local recruiting office for all branches. At that time he was issued a Defence Pass (*Wehrpaß*): a small booklet with his personal information and pre-military training record. The summer prior to his induction, usually at age 20, he would receive notification of his pending autumn call-up. He would take a physical at that time. After graduating from *Gymnasium* (six-year secondary school) in September he would receive his call-up letter telling him when and where to report and what documents to bring, including HJ and RAD records. Men were called up by their year class (*Jahrgang*). They could volunteer as early as 17 years of age.

Prior to the war there were numerous exemptions available for schooling, professions critical to military production, compassionate reasons (ill or elderly parents to care for, for example), or fathers of large families. From 1943 exceptions were greatly curtailed and even sole surviving sons of families were conscripted as well as younger and older classes of men called up.

5.5m medium inflatable boats are loaded with troops. It was these boats that were paddled across countless rivers to secure the far shore and allow a bridgehead to be established enabling the pioneers to build bridges and operate ferries.
(Nik Cornish at Stavka)

Crossing a pontoon bridge at night, under the supervision of the *Pioniere* during an exercise (note the coloured bands on helmets and caps). Brückengerät B bridge construction was a rather complicated procedure that required a reconnaissance of the area to determine the most suitable site to build the bridge and determine the type of bridge required. The Brückengerät B pontoon bridge sections could be assembled in three different configurations: a 130m-long version with a maximum capacity of 4 tons, an 80m-long version with a capacity of 8 tons, and a 50m-long version that could carry up to 20 tons. (Carlo Pecchi archive)

Peacetime conscription was for two years, after which an individual was reassigned to *Reserve I*, liable for call-up for short training periods and mobilization until age 35. It was this group that was called up to rapidly expand the army on the eve of the war. At age 45 individuals were transferred to *Landwehr I* and then *Landsturm I*. Those classified unfit or granted various exemptions were assigned to *Ersatzreserve I* or *II* and then to *Landwehr II* and *Landsturm II* at the appropriate ages.

When ordered to report for active service young men's families celebrated his going away with a formal dinner and party. Friends would also throw small parties. It was an honour for many families. However, not all were so enthusiastic. There were many who did not embrace the Nazis, and even more who vividly remembered the horror of the trenches and what war had brought to Germany. Prior to the encouragement of the Nazis to produce larger families, it was not uncommon for couples to have only one to three children. The departure of sons was often a sad occasion, even though the son himself may have been enthusiastic.

Recruits were selected for the pioneers based on related civilian skills: carpenters, framers, masons, road-workers, bridge-builders, loggers, those familiar with power equipment, and similar. General labourers and unskilled persons could find themselves wielding a pick and shovel as well.

Two pioneers rush forward in training carrying an extended charge (*Gestreckteladung*) as their *Unteroffizier* looks on. This consisted of 200g charges wired to planks at 10–15cm (4–6in.) intervals. (Nik Cornish at Stavka)

TRAINING

The basic training for a German infantryman of the period is well described in Osprey Warrior 59: *German Infantryman (1) 1933–40*, David Westwood (Osprey: Oxford, 2002). The initial 16-week basic training (*Grundausbildung*) period for a pioneer was essentially the same as an infantryman's. As the war wore on training was reduced to 12 weeks, and later to eight.

Reporting for duty was a formal occasion and recruits wore a coat and tie. They went through another physical, received a haircut, and were issued uniforms by their second or third day. Their civilian attire was

This pioneer squad's machine-gun troop has taken up position in a gap cut through the barbed wire and is providing cover fire with their MG.34 as the shock troop advances on the target. (Courtesy of Concord Publications)

mailed home. Recruits (*Rekruten*) were assigned to a pioneer replacement battalion (*Pioneer-Ersatz-Bataillon*). They would see very few officers. An *Unterfeldwebel* or *Feldwebel* usually ran their platoon (*Zug*), sometimes a recalled World War I (*Weltkrieg*) veteran.

Recruits knew training and discipline would be harsh and exacting under such tutorage. What they were not prepared for was the room elder (*Stubenalteste*). Eight men were assigned to a room to form a *Korporalschafts* or corporal's unit (*Schaft* in the military context means 'column'). Four such groups formed a *Zug*. This group would live, mess, and train together. The room elder was a *Gefreiter* or *Obergefreiter*, usually nearing the end of his two years' service. They were selected for their ability to instil and maintain discipline and were not above harassment, often cruelly so. They also had practical duties. They were to ensure their 'foals' (*Fohlen*) were ready for training and assembled on time. He taught them the many small details of military life such as making their beds, stowing and displaying their uniforms and equipment for inspection, how to clean their rifle and equipment, and ensured that room duties were performed: lights were turned off, windows and shutters closed, beds made, the room cleaned, the stove cleaned and extinguished when leaving, coal stocked, and that bed linen was turned in and drawn weekly. He also gave after-hours remedial instruction and ensured the recruits undertook their studies. He soon took away any thunder and ideas of independence a *Hammel* (castrated ram) may have deonstrated – a recruit who was said to be all bleat and no balls – a lot of talk, but no experience.

Training was practical and based on battle drills and typical routines soldiers would face in combat. While there were some things done by numbers – drill for example – combat actions were performance oriented. Soldiers were taught to immediately obey orders, but they were taught too to be flexible and to think for themselves if alone or finding themselves in a group without NCOs or officers present. Instilling this initiative served two purposes: it taught self-sufficiency and flexibility in combat, and developed future leaders. It is very difficult to later turn robot-like, blindly obedient soldiers who were taught not to think for themselves into effective decision-making leaders.

A **RIFLE DRILL IN A PIONEER REPLACEMENT BATTALION**

It was a challenge to keep the white drill uniform *(Drillichzug)* pristine and over time they took on a dingy faint greyish or yellowish tint to signify an old hand, an *alten Landser* ('old salt'). In 1940 reed green *Drillichzugen* began to be issued and the old white outfits became even more of a sign of veterans. The drill uniform was devoid of *Lametta* (tinsel), that is, insignia and adornments. Recruits did a great deal of rifle drill which improved physical fitness, stamina, coordination, and familiarity with the rifle, here Mauser Kar.98b 'carbines' issued to training and other second-line units. Being pioneers, they sometimes conducted such drills with shovels. Their *Obergefreiter*, wearing *Drillichhose*, drills them relentlessly, harassing them with *Schikanen* (nasty tricks). In the background is a Hf.1 light field wagon* with each *Pionierezug* possessing one for its equipment, which could weigh up to 1,360kg. Most wagons had smaller front wheels, but German military wagons used the same sized large wheels on all axels requiring only one size for replacements.

* Hf. = *Heersfahrzeug* (Army vehicle).

The pioneers made use of Goliath remotely controlled demolition charge carriers. There were two types, the Sd.Kfz.302 with two electric motors and controlled by a cable, pictured here, and the Sd.Kfz.303 with a gasoline engine, which was radio-controlled. The Sd.Kfz.302 carried 36kg (80lb) of demolitions. The first unit to receive these was Pionier-Bataillon (motorisiert) 'Taifun' (Typhoon) z.b.V. 600 and its Panzer-Pionier-Kompanien (Goliath) 811–815. The little carriers, known to the Allies as 'Doodlebugs', were employed to breach obstacles, destroy fortifications, and attack enemy armoured vehicles. (Nik Cornish at Stavka)

Recruits were taught how to use the rifle, machine gun, grenades, and bayonet. Marksmanship training and firing practice were extensive. Training also included individual movement and camouflage skills, map reading, use of the compass, range estimation, selecting movement routes, reporting battlefield information, gas mask drill, protection from gas attack, defence against aircraft with small arms, digging and camouflaging fighting positions, and field craft.

They were pushed hard with long training hours often lasting into the night. They were taught that physical and metal exhaustion, limited food, and lack of sleep could not and would not hamper their performance, encapsulated in the mantra: *Schweiß spart Blut* (sweat saves blood).

The training day began at 0500hrs, and sometimes earlier when they were roused out for unexpected country runs. They had to clean up, organize their room, prepare for training, and finish their limited breakfast by 0700hrs. The day usually began with calisthenics, rifle drills, or runs with full equipment called *bimsen* (bounding) – hard drill and practice. Almost every day there was some form of political indoctrination, lectures on history as seen by the Nazis, discussion of news events, lectures by local party officials, films, and similar.

Lectures on military training were kept to a minimum. Recruits would receive a short lecture and demonstration, then they would perform the action either on the drill field or in a field training area. Training films were used extensively to show how actions were accomplished and then practiced in the field. Later in the war, training films were very realistically portrayed. US and British training films tended to show soldiers in combat wearing uniforms of a parade ground quality and with every equipment strap in place. Soldiers in fighting positions would not flinch or even glance in the direction of nearby explosions. To anyone who had experienced combat such films were laughably unrealistic. German films depicted unshaven soldiers in dirty uniforms, but with all their equipment and otherwise in good order. They did flinch at explosions and were obviously nervous as enemy tanks approached. The idea was to demonstrate what combat was like and that it was all right to be frightened, but if one held one's ground, remained alert, and followed one's leader's orders, then they could prevail.

After lunch there was usually a brief inspection and more training followed. Unless there was night training scheduled the training day ended at 1830hrs with dinner. There was still work to be done in regards to studying

Ausgabe für der Pionier (*Issue for Pioneers* – 'issue' as in a publication) and *Ausbildungstaseln für der Pionier* (*Training Digest for Pioneers*), instruction by the *Gefreiter*, and *Putz und Flickstunde* (clean and patch hour), a time designated for cleaning and making clothing repairs.

Rather than sprawling military bases with ranges and training areas near the cantonment area, the Germans based troops in *Kaserne*, relatively small facilities with barracks, workshops, administrative buildings, a drill ground, and so on. They were located in and around towns and cities. Usually, a division's regiments and battalions each had their own *Kaserne* in the division's home city. Some kilometres away would be one or more troop training areas (*Truppenübungsplatz*) with firing ranges and tactical manoeuvre areas. Recruits would march to the training areas and to conserve training time they might remain there for several days or even a week or more. This too was part of their training as they lived in field conditions, either in 12-man tents (six if provided with folding cots), or more often they assembled four-man tents by buttoning their shelter-quarters together.

There was little actual pioneer-related instruction, other than more trench digging and building of field fortifications than infantrymen experienced (see Osprey Fortress 23: *German Field Fortifications 1939–45*, Gordon Rottman, Osprey: Oxford, 2004). The training very much emphasized infantry skills. Once basic was completed the troops were assigned to pioneer battalions where they would receive intense instruction on the many pioneer skills. Selected pioneers would be sent to technical schools.

In their unit over the next months they learned a wide variety of skills from experienced NCOs and officers: erecting various types of barbed-wire entanglements and fences, planting and erecting anti-tank and anti-personnel mines, constructing squad bunkers, machine-gun bunkers and other small fighting positions, use of inflatable boats, assembling pontoon and float bridges, erecting small timber bridges for light vehicles and personnel, building corduroy roads, repairing roads and small bridges, learning how to use hand tools and the limited types of power tools, camouflage techniques, road reconnaissance, rigging electrically and non-electrically initiated demolition charges, and more.

A significant part of the training was oriented to the assault aspect of the pioneers (see Osprey Elite 160: *World War II Infantry Assault Tactics*, Gordon Rottman, Osprey: Oxford, 2008). This meant extensive training and practice

Pioneers lay timbers on the roof of a completely subsurface troop quarters bunker. Waterproofing materials, if nothing else but a layer of clay, will top the timber roof and then the earth will be back-filled and camouflaged. (Nik Cornish at Stavka)

exercises breaching barbed-wire obstacles with various types of demolition charges and wire-cutters, employing smoke candles and grenades to blind the enemy and screen their own movements, use of supporting weapons, particularly the machine gun and flame-thrower, and use of different types of demolition charges to destroy enemy bunkers.

A pioneer squad (*Pioniergruppe*) would be attached to an infantry rifle platoon (*Schützezug*) when heavy defences and formidable obstacles were expected. The pioneers would provide their expertise with obstacle breaching, demolitions, smoke, and flame-throwers. The infantry were taught these assault skills too (with the exception of the flame-thrower) but the pioneers reinforced the infantry with their specialist skills. The infantry supported the attack with heavy machine guns, mortars, and infantry guns.

B **PIONEER NCO ASPIRANT**

A *Pionier Unteroffizier Awärter* was uniformed no differently than a *Rekrut* other than a 9mm-wide silver-coloured braid loop at the base of his shoulder straps (**1** and **2**). An *Unteroffizier Awärter* received the same pay as a *Gefreiter* and wore the single chevron on the left sleeve. He wears the shoulder straps of *Pionierschule I* in Berlin-Karlshorst. The stone grey trousers were issued in 1936 and began to be replaced by field grey in early 1940. This soldier carries the standard equipment used by infantrymen: steel helmet, belt, two 30-round cartridge pouches, bread bag, water bottle with drinking cup, gasmask carrier, and bayonet with the company-coloured tassel. The 'Y' support straps are not worn, but detachable wire belt hooks in the tunic's back were relied on to support the belt equipment. He is armed with a Kar.98b carbine, a weapon often used to equip training units. The black edge-piped shoulder straps are of a (left) pioneer battalion and (right) a pioneer school (**3**); their black embroidered numbers are edged by white stitching. The 54-page *Wehrpaß* (Defence Pass) (**4**) was issued when recruits were given their first pre-conscription physical and was a military service record retained by the company. The *Soldbuch* (Pay Book) (**5**) was a 24-page very detailed service record usually carried on the individual. These proved valuable to intelligence personnel if the soldier was captured. Each soldier carried small and large *Verbandpäckchen* (wound dressings) or *Faden abstreifen* (cloth strips) (**6**) in an inside tunic pocket. The *Erkennungsmarke* (identification tag) was commonly carried in a leather envelope (**7**) suspended by a neck cord. A chessboard *(Schachbrett)* with punch-out cardboard pieces (**8**) came with an envelope to mail it to soldiers. The 268-page *Ausgabe für der Pionier (Issue for Pioneers)* (**9**) was the standard pioneer soldier's manual; called a *Reibert* after the publisher, which printed manuals for all branches. It was supplemented by the 444-page *Pionierdienst aller Waffen (Pioneer Service for all Arms)* (**10**). The carbine cleaning kit *(Reinigungsgerät 34)* (**11**) held a chain pull-through, oil container, takedown tool, bore cleaning and oiling brushes, and bore cleaning tuff. A 15-round 7.9mm rifle cartridge carton (**12**) held three five-round loading clips (indicated by an overprinted red 'i.L.' *(im Ladestriefen)*. The practice stick grenade (Stielhandgranate 24, Übungs) (**13**) contained a small charge that generated a puff of white smoke through eight vent holes. It was more often used for throwing practice without the charge.

The pioneers and infantry would organize into three elements to breach obstacles and attack a bunker or small fortified complex. Their size varied depending on the obstacles, defences, and their layout. The covering troop (*Deckungstrupp*) placed suppressive fire on the targeted enemy position and adjacent positions. It may have been divided into small elements to adequately place fire on different positions. The covering troops would also manoeuvre around the objective to provide the most effective fire. The shock troop (*Stosstrupp*) was the assault element and would breach the obstacles at a point that avoided direct fire from the bunker. The shock troop was often composed entirely of pioneers. The smoke troop (*Nebeltrupp*) would position itself upwind of the breach point and targeted bunker. It would ignite smoke candles and grenades to blind the enemy and cover the movements of the shock troop. This element would also blind adjacent enemy positions. The shock troop would breach the barriers with demolitions and wire-cutters and then close in to attack the bunker with demolitions. They would blast the embrasures and place demolition charges on doors to blow them open. A flame-thrower might be employed to attack the embrasure and burn out the bunker if necessary.

RANK

In the first days of the new recruits' training they received instruction on identifying rank and insignia and the many rank titles, which varied between branches; there were also numerous specialist rank categories. The lowest ranks up through the *Gefreiter* grades all wore plain shoulder straps and were classified as enlisted men (*Mannschaften*). The lowest rank, the recruit, was a *Pionier*, equivalent to an infantry *Schütze* – rifleman. Individuals were appointed[1] to *Oberpionier* (senior pioneer) after six months to one year in service. It was generally granted to individuals who had not achieved *Gefreiter* during the same timeframe. The *Oberpionier* and *Gefreiter* grades were not reflected in manning tables and were not tied to duty positions. An *Oberpionier* was identified by a four-pointed star (*Stern*) on a cloth disc centred on the upper left sleeve. There were no appointments to this grade between 1936 and 1938.

Gefreiter was granted to individuals demonstrating leadership abilities and these pioneers were identified by a single point-down chevron. The *Gefreiter* grades are sometimes thought of as 'corporals' based on the chevrons, but they are simply senior privates first class. They held no actual leadership positions; their appointment was tied to time in service and merit. Individuals selected for NCO training were promoted to *Gefreiter* and additionally displayed a 9mm-wide silver-coloured braid loop on the base of their shoulder straps identifying them as an *Unteroffizier-Anwärter* (NCO candidate).

Soldiers were eligible for *Obergefreiter* after two years, but a *Gefreiter* could be promoted directly to *Unteroffizier* in wartime. An *Obergefreiter* was known as an *Oberschnäpser* (drunken waiter) in jest. In October 1936 two categories of *Obergefreiter* were established: *Obergefreiter weniger als 6 Dienstjahren* (with less than six years' service) identified by two chevrons and *Obergefreiter mit mehr als 6 Dienstjahren* (with over six years' service)

1. Soldiers were 'appointed' to *Oberpionier* and the *Gefreiter* grades and these were not considered 'promotions' (*Beförderung*). *Gefreiter* is derived from the Old German *gefreit* (counted) – one who paid homage (*huldigte*) to local sovereigns, a loyal vassal.

displaying a single chevron with a star. Those with fewer than six years' service might eventually be promoted to *Unteroffizier*. Those with over six years were considered unfit for NCO leadership duties with little chance of promotion – *die ewigen Gefrieter* (the eternal *Gefreiter*). It was basically a pay increase for time in service and not for merit. *Stabsgefreiter* was identified by two chevrons and a star. This was an individual with an administrative assignment, clerical in nature. Appointments to *Stabsgefreiter* ceased in October 1934, but individuals remained in the rank for some time and it was re-established in April 1942.

NCO ranks were identified by 9mm-wide braid edging the shoulder straps, except *Unteroffizier*, which had an open base end, and 9mm braid around the tunic collar. The length of time in service and time in grade as well as completed examinations, demonstrated skills, and merit determined promotion. This was of course abbreviated in wartime.

The *Unteroffizier* was a squad leader (*Gruppeführer*) equating to a British and US corporal. It was sometimes referred to as *Kapo* (headman). Promotion to the lowest of the NCO grades required graduation from an NCO school or two years' service with one year as a *Gefreiter* in wartime. NCO ranks did not necessarily have to be progressively obtained; grades could be skipped.

An *Unteroffizier* squad leader leads his men down a trench carrying small 16in.-long wire-cutters. (Courtesy of Concord Publications)

An *Unterfeldwebel* was usually a platoon troop leader (*Führer des Zugtrupps*), equivalent to a platoon sergeant, but this position could be held by a *Feldwebel* too. These two ranks both required at least two years as an *Unteroffizier* and six years' total service. These two grades could also lead sections, other elements, or be assigned to staffs. There was no specified time

as an *Unterfeldwebel* prior to promotion to *Feldwebel* (translated as 'sergeant'. *Feld* prefixed to a word often connotes a military meaning. *Webel* is an Old German term for 'usher'). *Oberfeldwebel* required seven years' service and at least one year as an *Unterfeldwebel* or *Feldwebel*. *Stabsfeldwebel* was reserved for long-career NCOs with over 12 years' service and no specified time in a prior grade. They were usually found in unit staffs. It was not uncommon for *Unterfeldwebelen* and higher to command platoons owing to officer shortages and they were even so designated on tables of organization.

The *Hauptfeldwebel*, sometimes listed along with NCO ranks, was an appointment rather than a rank. It was the equivalent of a US company first sergeant or British company sergeant-major, the senior NCO in the company – the 'reporting NCO' responsible for troop accountability and administration. He was commonly referred to as *der Spieß* (the pike), reminiscent of the day when sergeants carried pikes to keep the troops in formation. As the company commander was known as the *Vater der Kompanie* (father of the company), the *Hauptfeldwebel* was the *Mutter der Kompanie* (mother of the company). A *Hauptfeldwebel* could be an *Unterfeldwebel*, *Feldwebel*, or *Oberfeldwebel* and was identified by two 9mm-wide braid cuff bands called *Kolbenringe* (piston rings) as well as a small leather report pouch (*Meldtasche*) tucked in his tunic opening and known as the 'prayer book' (*Gebetsbuch*) as soldiers prayed their name would not be entered in it.

Individuals were addressed by their rank preceded by *Herr*, for example, *Herr Pionier, Herr Feldwebel, Herr Leutnant*. The traditional hand salute used by the Wehrmacht was the right hand touching the forehead or cap/helmet visor. The *Hitlergruß* (Hitler salute) – formally the *Deutschesgruß* (German salute) long used by the Nazis – was ordered as the only salute authorized in the Wehrmacht on 24 July 1944, accompanied by 'Heil Hitler' or 'Sieg Heil' (hail to victory), after the 20 July assassination attempt on Hitler. This was in the form of the outstretched right arm at an angle of 45 degrees. Its mandatory use was not favourably received by many troops.

Pioneer troops board a 5.5m inflatable boat to conduct a reconnaissance. It was one matter to select a bridge crossing site on the near side of a river, but several additional questions needed answering: is there a suitable exit site on the far side; are there marshes or swamps on the far side; is the far bank too steep; is the ground firm enough for a road; is there a nearby existing road network reachable from the river? (Nik Cornish at Stavka)

DAILY LIFE

German barracks were comfortable and provided all necessary amenities. The two- or three-storey monolithic structures were robustly built of brick or concrete with tile roofs (many are still in use today). They had double-glazed windows and usually central heating in the form of steam radiators heated by coal-fired boilers. Most rooms held eight men although some older barracks had large bays. There were also two- and four-man rooms for NCOs depending on their grade. Sometimes double bunks were used, but mostly there were single beds. Each man had a spacious two-door wooden wall locker (see Plate C). The latrines were well lit and provided with sinks, mirrors, toilets, trough urinals, and shower rooms. Hot water was available, but owing to wartime fuel shortages was often cut off.

The barracks included administrative offices, supply rooms, storage areas, arms rooms, kitchens, mess halls with separate dining rooms for NCOs and other ranks, recreation rooms, and sitting rooms for reading and study. Some barracks had basements and some of these rooms were located there along with the heating boiler.

Combination motorcycles with sidecars are being ferried across a river in France by *Pioniere* using a raft built using four medium rubber boats. Such makeshift solutions could only work with light equipment or small vehicles and were not suitable for any assault crossing since only paddles could be used. Larger rafts were made using pontoon bridge sections, these being suitable for heavy vehicles and equipment. (Pier Paolo Battistelli)

Order, routine, and cleanliness were demanded. Recruits learned what really made an army work: orderliness and punctuality. *Ordnung muß sein!* (Everything must be in order) was a slogan often seen on signs in barracks as a reminder to keep things straight, clean, and organized. A similar slogan was *Alles in Ordnung* (All in order) meaning everything should be in its place. *Fünf Minuten vor der Zeit, ist Soldatenpünktlichkeit* (Five minutes ahead of time is soldierly punctuality) was another slogan often seen and heard in barracks as a reminder to be on time, always.

Besides discipline inflicted by the NCOs there was also a degree of self-policing. There were always soldiers who did not fit in, whose misbehaviour or mistakes led to group punishment. The rest of the soldiers might collectively beat the offender in a night-time attack. When asked who conducted the attack the barracks would reply, '*Der Heilige Geist*' (the Holy Ghost).

For diversion on the *Kasern*, a *Kantine* (canteen) was provided. Beer, coffee, hot tea, apple juice, and Fanta (Fanta was introduced in Germany in 1940, was very popular, and was apple flavoured) were common drinks. Schnapps, cognac, and wine were sometimes available. *Kaffee und Kuchen* (coffee and cakes), *Bratwurst und Brötchen* (sausage and bread rolls), *Bratwurst und Sauerkraut* (sausage and sauerkraut), and *Schupfnudeln* (potato noodles) were popular snacks along with candy and pastries. *Lebkuchen* (gingerbread), *Stollen* (fruit bread), and other treats were served on holidays. Units might establish a *Feldkantine* (field canteen) behind their front lines in quiet sectors. Also available was a *Krämer* (shop), the unit store (*Marketenderei*), which sold toiletries, tobacco, personal need items, writing materials, and so on.

Meals were served in spacious well-lit dining rooms family-style, with platters and bowls passed from man-to-man with each serving themselves. In some instances, containers of food would be brought to each barracks

A *Baupioniere* (construction engineer) unit at work on a road somewhere on the southern portion of the Eastern Front, during the summer of 1942. As a general rule all the bridging equipment used by the advancing divisions during their march was subsequently removed and replaced by more permanent works (often made of wood or stone) built later by the construction engineers. (Carlo Pecchi archive)

room by detailed men and eaten on the room table. As in any army soldiers were detailed to work in the kitchen under the *Küchenbulle* (kitchen bull), the cook (*Koch*) helping to prepare food and clean eating and cooking utensils in the form of *Küchendienst* (kitchen service).

Garrison food was simple but nutritional, and for the most part found acceptable by the troops. Breakfast (*Frühstück*) was very light. Instead of the American concept of breakfast being the most important meal of the day, the Germans believed that since soldiers had done nothing all night but sleep they had not 'earned' a full meal. It typically consisted of bread and boiled potatoes with coffee. Coffee was served in uninsulated steel pitchers meaning it was seldom served hot. The midday meal (*Mittagessen*), the day's largest, was normally stew or sausage and bread, often with potatoes or some other vegetable such as peas or beans (there are many references to 'legumes' (*Leguminosen*), which is a vegetable category inclusive of peas and beans). Supper (*Abendbort*) was often soup and bread. Butter, marmalade, and other spreads were available for bread. Soups and stews included meat (beef, pork,

BARRACKS WALL LOCKER

The pioneer soldier's wall locker (*Spind*) was his repository for all issue clothing and equipment as well as the few personal items permitted. It was precisely arranged, the exact arrangement varying between units, and was to be ready for inspection at any time. The helmet and backpack (**1**) were stowed on top. On the top shelf of the main compartment (**2**) were neatly stacked shirts, under drawers, socks, nightshirts and sweater, along with the field cap. On a hanger bar (**3**) are the drill, field, and service tunics and trousers, and greatcoat. On the main compartment's left-side wall are hung equipment items with more on the door, along with a towel (**4**). Shoes and boots are stowed on the bottom shelf and beneath it (**5**). To the left of the main compartment are seven small compartments containing (from top to bottom): peaked service cap (**6**); bread for the day's meals, eating utensils, plate, soup bowl, saucer, cup (compartment has door) (**7**); personal items and valuables (locked door) (**8**); toiletries (razor, blades, shaving stick, toothbrush, toothpowder, soap, comb) (**9**); manuals, books, writing materials (**10**); cleaning materials (leather polish, shoe and cleaning brushes, cleaning cloths) (**11**); gasmask, mess kit, and *Zeltbahn* shelter-quarter (**12**). Photos and personal letters might have been permitted to be attached inside the left compartment's door (**13**).

A camouflaged 15cm s.F.H. heavy field howitzer loaded on a pontoon ferry. A Sturmboot 39 is used to propel the ferry. This photograph provides a view of the assault boat's 'mechanical oar'. (Nik Cornish at Stavka)

chicken, fish) and vegetables. Cheese and puddings were commonly served. Fresh fruit was rare, often being served only for holiday meals. Bread was issued in the largest quantity by weight, followed by potatoes, and then vegetables. Meat and fish were far down the issue scale.

Soldiers were granted various categories of leave (*Urlaub*): *Wochenendurlaub* (weekend), *Kurzurlaub* (short four-day), *Festtagsurlab* (holiday), *Sonderurlaub* (special), *Einsatzurlaub* (pre-deployment), *Genesungurlaub* (convalescence), and *Lehrgangsurlaub*. The latter provided travel time leave for soldiers in transit to training schools and in peacetime sometimes allowed a visit home.

Pay day was much anticipated by all soldiers. While American soldiers were paid on the last Friday of the month, the *Landser* looked forward to three paydays (*Zahltag*): the 1st, 11th, and 21st. The *Wehrsold* (defence pay or basic pay) was made in three equal payments even though there were eight to 11 days remaining in the month, if not engaged in combat. Besides basic pay soldiers received *Frontzulage* (front pay), a form of 'combat pay', which varied by rank. It was paid with the basic pay, but a fixed amount was paid per day.

Basic pay for a *Pionier* was RM30 (US$12), a *Gefreiter* RM34 (US$14), and a *Feldwebel* RM40 (US$18). Troops were often paid in Wehrmacht script or the currency of the country they were in. Pay was doled out by the *Zahlmeister* (paymaster) known to his 'clients' as a *Zahlmops* (literally 'number pug' or 'money pincher'). Pay could be deposited in a savings account at home.

Troops were encouraged to write home often and this was a common pastime. Letters were heavily censored in wartime. It was forbidden to speak of unit designations, locations, movements, weapons, equipment, treatment of local civilians, or even mention casualties. They were not to complain of conditions or of the war and certainly there was to be no political commentary. On the home front civilians were told not to write to the soldiers complaining of conditions, food shortages, and the incessant bombing. It was reasoned that discouraging news from home would cause concern to the soldiers and distract them from concentrating on their mission, as well as reducing their morale.

APPEARANCE

In the field a pioneer looked little different from his infantry counterpart. There were three means of differentiating a *Pionier* from a *Stopplehopser* (stubble-hopper): infantry had white *Waffenfarbe* (arm of service colour) piping edging their shoulder straps and pioneers had black, the pioneers were often muddier than the infantrymen, if that is possible, and pioneers carried bigger shovels.

Black uniform distinctions in the form of shoulder straps, shoulder strap piping, collar and cuff patch piping, and so on depending on the period have been worn by the pioneers since 1808 when Prussian pioneers adopted the colour. Enlisted men had their unit number embroidered in black on shoulder straps (NCOs wore silver-coloured devices and officers gold-coloured). On dark bluish-green shoulder straps the black devices were difficult to see, so they were edged with white stitching. Pioneer battalion flags had a black background.

A pioneer shock troop closes in on an enemy log bunker. In the foreground is a Flammerwerfer 35 flame-thrower. (Nik Cornish at Stavka)

German *Baupioniere* at work repairing a destroyed bridge; they are all wearing the white denim fatigue uniform that, along with the setting and the kind of work undertaken, suggests that this is in a rear area well after the fighting has finished. (Pier Paolo Battistelli)

The daily duty uniform was the *Feldzug*, which consisted of the field tunic and trousers made of a wool and polyester blend in a deep warm olive green belying its field grey (*Feldgrau*) name. As the war wore on the amount of polyester increased, giving it a less smart appearance and reducing its warmth. The fabric tended to 'fade' to more greyish shades. The collar and shoulder straps were dark bluish-green. Most cloth uniform insignia were backed with this same badge cloth. Boots, belts, and other leather gear were black. The *Feldzug* included the steel helmet and combat equipment. Without these items, other than the belt and with the addition of the field cap, it became the service uniform (*Dienstzug*).

D   CONTENTS OF THE BACKPACK AND BREAD BAG

The backpack (Tornister 34) was designed to contain a precise list of items. This design principle dated back to another era when warfare was conducted on a seasonal basis supported by regular supply. Field conditions in World War II demanded that units operate more independently and troops needed to carry additional rations and cold weather clothing. Battle rucksacks began to replace the backpack in 1941 in combat units. The basic contents remained much the same, but with additions. (**1**) Shaving kit, wash kit, sewing kit. (**2**) Underwear and towel. (**3**) Socks. (**4**) Rolled greatcoat. (**5**) Right laced-top shoe. (**6**) Mess kit. (**7**) Mess kit cover. (**8**) Left laced-top shoe. (**9**) Tent rope. (**10**) Carbine cleaning kit. (**11**) Half iron ration meat can.

The bread bag (Brotbeutel 31) carried essential personal immediate need items in the field, in addition to the daily bread ration. In 1944 a pocket was added on the bag's right, under the flap for the carbine cleaning kit. Individual preference dictated its contents, which might include: (**12**) Esbit field stove (open and folded), (**13**) Esbit fuel tablets, (**14**) fat box (for cooking-fat or butter), (**15**) eating utensils (assembled and disassembled). Many carried only a spoon and an issue can opener (**16**). The field cap and perhaps a pair of socks might be carried.

Examples of personal items carried in the backpack or rucksack include: (**17**) razor and blades, (**18**) shaving stick, (**19**) toothbrush, (**20**) toothpowder, (**21**) soapbox, (**22**) comb, (**23**) foot powder, and (**24**) pocketknife.

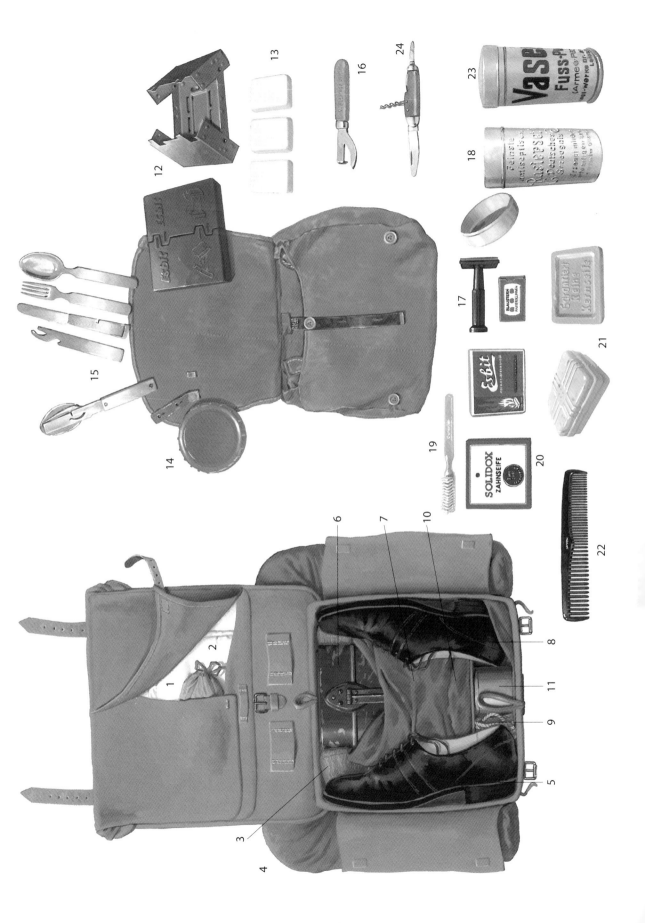

Another daily uniform was the drill uniform (*Drillichzug*), a white denim outfit worn on work details with the field grey field cap. A more practical reed green version began to be issued in 1940. Marching boots (*Marschstiefel*) – *Knobelbecher* (toss-pots as in tossing dice) or *Würfelbecher* (dice-shakers) – were a signature component of the German uniform, but in mid-1942 the low laced-top boots (*Schnuursteifel*) came into increased use coupled with canvas gaiters called retreat gaiters (*Rückzugs-Gamaschen*) owing to the legend that when they were issued the war was lost.

German soldiers were typically 165cm (5ft 5in.) to 178cm (5ft 10in.) tall, but there is evidence that pioneers were typically shorter as taller troops tended to be assigned to the infantry. On average, German soldiers were 5cm (2in.) shorter than Americans. Recruits' hair was cut very short, although left a little longer on top. This practice was continued after basic training, but left still longer on top. Moustaches were very rare.

Individual equipment

Pioneers were issued basically the same gear as the infantry. It was a proud day, second only to when they were issued their rifles, when recruits received their *Feldausrüstung des Mannes*, or field equipment for men (see Osprey Men-at-Arms 234, *German Combat Equipments 1939–45*, Gordon Rottman, Osprey: Oxford, 1991). The equipment was made of black leather, field grey (dark green) fabric, and field grey-painted metal. As the war progressed, the fabric and paint colours varied greatly as did stopgap gear of increasingly shoddy construction. Substitute materials and webbing replaced many previously leather items. Soldiers spent as much time cleaning and maintaining their equipment as they did weapons and uniforms.

A *Pionier* unit is crossing a river using a footway built on a collapsed concrete bridge during the campaign against France, 1940. The *Pioniere* are carrying their equipment over their shoulders, which was the only solution possible at this early stage of the river crossing. (Pier Paolo Battistelli)

The basic kit consisted of the leather belt with support straps (Y-straps), a pair of three-pocket cartridge pouches (each pocket holding two five-round clips for 30 rounds), entrenching tool and bayonet on the left side, and the bread bag over the right hip. The water bottle and sometimes the cook pot would be attached to D-rings on the bread bag. The robust steel gasmask case was slung over the right shoulder and the can-like container went over the bread bag. The anti-gas sheet packet was fastened to the gasmask case's strap on the chest. Often it was strapped around the case itself. The watertight case often served as a repository for cigarettes, matches, socks, letter writing materials, and so on, resulting it becoming known as the *Zigarettenbüchse* (cigarette box).

The bread bag, almost as much of a distinctive item of the German soldier as the 'coal scuttle' helmet, jackboots, and fluted gasmask case, carried a number of frequently needed items: the field cap, socks, smoking pipe, pocket folding field stove, fuel tablets, fat box (for cooking-fat or butter), meat container (for bacon or sausage), eating utensils, and the next meal's rations, including bread (see Plate D).

The Flammerwerfer 35 was one of the more commonly used models of flame-thrower, and was based on the World War I M.16. The smaller tank contains the compressed nitrogen (*Stickstoff-Druckgas*) propellant. A special acid-resistant synthetic material suit was issued to flame-gunners to protect from fuel blowback. Burning fuel would quickly melt the material. It did not appear to be too much of a concern as the suits were seldom worn. This *Gefreiter* even has his sleeves rolled up. (Courtesy of Concord Publications)

The Tornister 34 was a small backpack with integral shoulder straps; its back flap was covered with unshaved calfskin as a means of waterproofing, resulting in it being called an *Affe* (ape). Later models lacked the calfskin. The M39 was similar, but lacked shoulder straps and may or may not have had the calfskin. It was carried attached to the infantry support straps. These backpacks proved inadequate for carrying additional rations and cold weather clothing. In late 1941 they began to be replaced by *Kampf Rucksacken* (battle rucksacks). These were larger rucksacks and most had two small pockets on the back. They may have had integral straps or lacked them, requiring attachment to support straps.

The prescribed contents of the backpack were: laced-top shoes, cook pot (with preserved bread inside), tent accessory pouch, carbine cleaning kit, socks, sweater in cold weather, sewing, shaving and washing kits (small drawstring cloth bags); towel, handkerchiefs, and undershirt. The greatcoat, blanket, and reversible camouflage shelter-quarter were secured to the outside as a horseshoe roll (see Plate D).

The Bekleidungssack 31 (clothing bag) was a small canvas satchel carried by the company baggage train. It might hold a drill uniform, underwear, socks, and tunic collar liners.

The steel helmet (Stahlhelm 35) was considered an equipment item. It was issued in six head sizes. The *Helm* was known variously as the *Blechhut* (tin hat), *Hurratüte* (hurrah party hat), and *Parteihut* (party hat). Besides its dark field grey paint, a number of means were used to enhance camouflage, attach camouflage materials, and break up its silhouette: canvas and burlap covers, cord nets, wire mesh, leather or web straps, and rubber bands made from tire inner-tubes. They were sometimes painted to match the terrain and seasonal colour such as desert sand, painted in a camouflage pattern, or whitewashed (in winter environments).

Recruits were issued a single *Erkennungsmarke* (identification tag) or *E-marke* or *Hundemarke* (dog tag), rather than two separate tags as the US and British armies provided. It was a 5 × 7cm (2 × 2.75in.) zinc, steel, or aluminium oval punched with three slits on its long axis. This allowed it to be snapped in two, with the one piece attached to the cord remaining with the body and the other turned in to the *Hauptfeldwebel*. Only three items of information were stamped on the two mirrored halves: the soldier's original training unit, his roster number (*Stammrollennummer*), and blood type. A pioneer's tag might have shown:

128   A
2.Kp./Pio.Ers.Btl.12

This means 'roster number 128, blood type A, 2nd Company, Pioneer Replacement Battalion 12' (2. Kompanie/Pionier-Ersatz-Bataillon 12). For comfort, the tag was often carried in a small cloth or leather envelope secured to a string, shoelace, or fine chain cord. This information was entered in the soldier's *Soldbuch* and *Wehrpaß* as well as on a consolidated company list, updated monthly. The information on turned-in tags was compared to the list for body identification. It made it difficult to identify bodies when recovering them in an area in which several units and their attachments had fought. If the tags were lost the replacement tag would reflect his new unit's identification. The company lists were forwarded and registered with the Armed Forces Information Office for Casualties and War Prisoners. One advantage of the system was that enemy intelligence could not usually identify the soldier's present parent unit. Late in the war simplified tags were issued with a five-digit field post number assigned to each unit and his roster number within the unit. The blood type was not always stamped.

In combat, soldiers were issued two *Verbandpäckchen* (wound dressings), 2cm-thick (0.8in.) field dressings wrapped in grey or green cloth secured by string. Unfolded, the smaller was 5 × 8.5cm (2 × 3.3in.) and the larger was 7 × 11cm (2.8 × 4.3in.) – entry and exit wound dressings respectively. These were carried in an inside pocket on the tunic's left skirt.

In the early stages of the Blitzkrieg, the use of bridging equipment was essential to enable German units to quickly cross every type of obstacle. Small streams and canals were the most common gap obstacles encountered. Here a makeshift pontoon bridge allows a 4-ton cargo truck to cross a small canal. (Carlo Pecchi archive)

Pioneer equipment

Pioneer hand tools included long- and short-handled spades. The short model had a leather cover for the blade that attached to the belt and was carried with the handle strapped to the pack. There was also a small pickaxe with a detachable head and a leather cover. Large (61cm or 24in.) and small (41cm or 16in.) heavy-duty wire-cutters had insulated handles to protect against electrical shock. There was also a 42cm-blade (16.5in.) handsaw with a leather scabbard. Unit hand tools included long-handled shovels, pickaxes, axes, hatchets, sledgehammers, augers, pry-bars, and two-man crosscut saws. Captured military and commandeered civilian tools were valued by pioneers to replace and supplement their own.

An item unique to the pioneers was the pioneer assault pack (*Pioniersturmgepäck*) issued on a basis of one for every five men. This worked out to two or three per squad, although they appear to have been little used, probably because they simply were not available to all units. Its production ran from early 1941 into 1944. It consisted of an assault pack carried on the back and two side pouches attached to the belt. It used the standard leather belt and Y-straps. The bayonet and water bottle were attached to the belt, but the side pouches prevented a bread bag from being carried. The three-compartment backpack held a mess kit, two Nb.K.39 smoke pots, and a 3kg demolition charge. The right-hand pouch held the gasmask and the left contained 100-gram, 200-gram, and 1kg charges. Both pouches had four pockets for five-round carbine clips.

Several types of electric igniter apparatus were in use, Glühzündapparat 26, 37, 39, and 40. These were detonating machines or exploders used to electrically fire charges. The ignition equipment kit (Zündgerät 40) held a Glühzündapparat 40, electrical circuit continuity testers, spools of single and double firing wire, electric detonators, insulating tape, and hand tools. The ignition tool kit (*Zünderwerkzeugtasche*) contained an assortment of small demolition tools in a leather case.

The Germans used a number of types of mine detectors (*Minensuchgerät*), which were designated by German city names: Aachen 40, Berlin 40, Frankfurt 40, Templehof 41, Wein 41, and Frankfurt 42. Since many mines were non-metallic, manual probing was often necessary. The 'mine-probing rod 39' was a two-section alloy tube with a steel spike point. Thin 2m-long steel rods were also used along with the standby bayonet.

Squad leaders and most other NCOs carried a report/map case, 6 × 30 universal binoculars, a march compass, a field pocket lamp (*Felftaschen Lampe*), and an army whistle (see Plate F).

Weapons

Pioneers used the same weapons as their infantry brothers. In the first days of training they were issued Mauser 7.9mm Kar.98b 'carbines'. This was simply an updated Gew.98 rifle as used in World War I. It was still rifle length at 125cm (49in.) rather than being a shorter carbine, and weighed 4kg (9lb). The recruits were told that the five-shot, bolt-action rifle was the best in the world, and indeed, the Mauser 1898 design was among the best. To the *Landser* his rifle (*Gewehr*) was known as the *Mauserbüchse* (*Büchse*, an old term for firearm), *Flinte* (shotgun), or *Knarre* (colloquialism for gun). They quickly learned never to call it by these names within hearing of instructors. They also called it the '*K acht und neunzig*' (K eight and ninety). Instructors referred to the rifle as the soldier's bride (*Soldatenbraut*), which, unlike a real wife, would never leave his side. With the rifle was issued the sidearm (*Seitengewehr*), or bayonet (*Bajonett*), a rarely used term. The S.84/98 had a blade 18–20cm (7–8in.) long and a steel scabbard (*Scheide*).

A *Sturmpionier* (assault engineer) posing with full equipment. He is wearing the pioneer assault pack (*Pioniersturmgepäck*). These were used to carry Stg.24 stick hand grenades and Nb.Hgr.39 smoke stick grenades or Eihgr.39 'egg grenades' as well as demolition charges. On the ground, to the right, is a *Pionier* spade with detachable handle and the top half of a 50kg hollow charge (the lower half being carried by another man). (Private collection)

Once assigned to a field army unit recruits would be issued the Mauser Kar.98k Karbiner, the standard shoulder arm since 1933. The *Mauserkarabiner* was a true carbine, being 111cm (43.6in.) in length and weighing 136g (0.3lb) less than the rifle. This was a rugged, solid, reliable weapon in which the *Landser* confidently placed his trust.

Here a cut is hand dug for a railroad siding. Pioneer units possessed no powered earthmoving equipment. (Nik Cornish at Stavka)

It was simple to operate. To load it the smoothly operating bolt was opened, a five-round charging clip inserted in the clip guides forward of the bolt, the cartridges pressed into the magazine with the thumb, and the bolt closed ejecting the clip. A small lever on the end of the bolt served as a safety, locking the rifle when switched to the right. The rear sight was graduated from 100–2,000m, but it was not very effective for accurate firing on a man-sized target over 500m away. The sight had no windage adjustment, so shooters had to learn to compensate on their own rifle. A leather sling was fitted to the weapon's left side.

A short cleaning rod was beneath the barrel and three rods screwed together were required to clean the bore. Each man was issued a cleaning kit (Reinigungsgerät 34) in a tin container. It had a lid on both ends, the large compartment holding a chain pull-through (in lieu of a cleaning rod), oil container, takedown tool, and bore cleaning and oiling brushes. In the other end was the bore cleaning tuff.

Pioneer units received a liberal allocation of 7.9mm MG.34 machine guns owning to their employment as assault troops and for self-defence. Each pioneer squad had a machine gun with a four-man crew, a secondary duty to their pioneer role. Production of this excellent, but expensive weapon began in 1936 and it went on to be considered one of the most effective machine guns of the era. The 122cm-long (48in.) weapon weighed 12kg (26½lb), making it slightly heavier than the light machine guns and automatic rifles used by other armies. It could be fired from the shoulder, underarm, or in the prone position from a bipod. To the *Landser* the *Einheitsmaschinengewehr* (universal machine gun) was known as the *Kaffeemühle* (coffee-grinder), *Dünnschißkanone* (diarrhoea cannon), *Gartenspritzer* (garden sprinkler), *Hitlersäge* (Hitler's saw), *Hitlergeige* (Hitler's violin), and *Schnatterpuste* (chatter breath) among others.

It spat out 800–900rpm, which sounded like ripping paper (most US and British automatics fired around 500rpm). After 250 rounds of high-rate fire the barrel was supposed to be swapped with one of two spares. In an emergency 400 rounds could be fired before changing. This was a simple matter of cocking the gun, setting it on safe (a button above the trigger on the left side), pushing in the receiver latch (left side below the sight), pivoting the receiver counter clockwise half a turn, lowering the receiver until the barrel slid out of the jacket, and removing it with an asbestos pad. The gun was levelled, the fresh barrel slid in, and the process reversed.

The crew was provided with a number of 50-round non-disintegrating metallic-linked belts. These were fastened together to make longer belts, but mainly they were loaded in a 50-round basket drum (Gurttrommel 34). Belts of 250 rounds were also available, mainly for anti-aircraft use, for which a high tripod was provided. The belts were part of the gun's accessories and were never discarded. Ammunition was issued in 1,500-round wooden boxes with five 300-round cartons containing 20 15-round cardboard packages.

Another view of a *Sturmpionier* with full equipment. On the ground (left to right) is a pole charge *(Stangenladung)* with a 3kg charge fastened to the end, two 3kg demolition charges with stick hand grenade handles attached, and a number of Stg.24 stick grenades. (Private collection)

A *Sturmpionier* posing with stick hand grenades, a 3kg demolition charge, large wire-cutters, and two sections of bangalore torpedoes (Rohrladung, Stahl, 3kg). (Private collection)

The crew had to link the ammunition. Two 50-round basket magazines were carried in a steel carrier called a Gurttromelträger 34. The crew carried two of these. A 250-round belt or six linked-together 50-round belts were carried in three steel or aluminium cartridge containers, the Patronenkasten 34 or 41.

Machine-gun crews and officers were issued Walther P.38 or Luger P.08 9mm pistols. Both had eight-round magazines. The 9mm MP.40 machine pistols were seldom issued to pioneers.

Grenades were widely used, including the common stick hand grenade 1924 (Stielhandgranate 24 – Stg.24) known as the 'potato-masher' (*Kartoffelstampfer*) or 'door-knockers' (*Türklopfer*) used to 'announce' one's entry into a building. A more conventional grenade was the small egg hand grenade 1939 (Eihandgranate 39 – Eihgr.39), the *Eierhandgranate* or a *Knackmandel* (almond in the shell). Later in the war the similar stick hand grenade 1943 (Stielhandgranate 43 – Stg.43) was introduced. Rather than having the fuse contained in the handle it was fitted with the same type of fuse atop the head as the egg grenade. These were all blast grenades relying on explosive effect and provided little fragmentation, but add-on fragmentation sleeves were available, though seldom used. All had a 4.5-second delay.

Smoke was an important weapon for pioneers during the assault. The smoke hand grenade 1939 (Nebelhandgranaten 39 – Nb.Hgr. 39) looked just like the Stg.24 stick grenade, but with a white band around the head. It generated dense white smoke for 100–120 seconds. The smoke egg hand grenade 1942 (Nebeleihandgranate 42 – Nb.Eihgr.42) had a more elongated and smaller diameter body than the Eihgr.39. The smoke fume cylinder 1939 (Rauchrohr Nebel 39) was a smoke candle consisting of a 2.5cm-diameter (1in.), 25cm-long (10in.) cylindrical metal tube intended to blind enemy tanks and bunkers. It emitted dark grey smoke for three to four minutes. A larger smoke-generating device was the smoke candle 1939 (Nebelkerzen 39 – Nb.K.39). This white smoke candle consisted of a 2.2kg (4.75lb) hand-emplaced can,

PIONEER DEMOLITIONS TRAINING

The pioneers employed both fabricated and field-expedient explosive devices. Here an *Unterfeldwebel* instructor, wearing the service uniform (*Dienstzug*), prepares a display of demolition devices. Fuses and detonators are not fitted in the charges other than 6 and 8. On the table (left to right) are: (**1**) 100g boring cartridge (Bohrpatrone 28), (**2**) 200g demolition container (Sprengkörper 28), (**3**) 1kg (2.2lb) demolition petard (Sprengbüchse 24), (**4**) 3kg (6.6lb) and (**5**) 10kg (22lb) concentrated charges (*Geballteladungen*), (**6**) 3kg ball charge (Kugelladung 3kg), (**7**) 12.5kg shaped-charge (Hohlladung 12.5kg), which could penetrate almost 7.6cm (3in.) of armour plate, (**8**) 3kg magnetic hollow charge (Haft-Hohlladung 3kg) – 'armour-cracker' (*Panzerknacker*) not introduced until late 1942, (**9**) concentrated charge (*Geballteladung*) made by wiring six Stg.24 stick grenade heads around a complete grenade, and (**10**) a double-charge (*Doppelladung*) comprised of two wired together 1kg demolition petards. Against the wall rest: (**11**) 3kg tube charge, steel (Rohrladung, Stahl, 3kg), (**12**) field fabricated extended charge (*Gestreckteladung*) with 200g charges, and (**13**) a field fabricated pole charge (*Stangenladung*) with a 3kg concentrated change wired to the end.

These two *Pioniere* carry the two sections of the 50kg hollow charge. When reaching the target, usually a fortification, the two sections would be assembled nesting together. The charge could penetrate almost 25cm (10in.) of armour plate. The soldier to the left is an *Oberpionier* and the other a *Gefreiter*. (Private collection)

German civilians view a mannequin of a *Pionier* carrying a Flammenwerfer 35 at a public display. The mannequin is wearing the two-piece flame-thrower protective suit (*Flammenwerfer-Schützanzug*) similar to that in use by the crews of the *Nebelwerfer* (rocket launcher) units. It included a tunic, trousers, and gauntlets of dark brown leather. Often facemasks with goggles were more often used rather than this face shield. A leather protective hood was also introduced, intended for use with a thick layer of grease to protect the face. Later in the war a one-piece leather overall protective suit was introduced, but since later models of flame-throwers were safer to use, special protective garments were no longer needed. (Private collection)

which was 14.6cm (5.7in.) tall, and 8.9cm (3.5in.) in diameter, with a wire carrying handle on top allowing the lid to be peeled off revealing a pull-type friction-igniter. It burned for four to seven minutes. Two of any of these devices could be connected by a short length of wire and thrown over tank or bunker gun barrels to blind the crew.

Besides demolition changes that could be configured into various types of special charges, two purpose-made charges were available. A little-used munition was the 16cm-diameter (6.29in.) 3kg ball charge (Kugel-Ladung 3kg). It was used like a satchel charge to throw through pillbox embrasures and fitted with a 7.5-second delay fuse. The 3kg magnetic hollow charge (Haft-Hohlladunge 3kg - Haft-Hl.3) known as the 'armour-cracker' (*Panzerknacker* – akin to a nutcracker) was a hand-emplaced, hollow-charge mine adopted in November 1942. It was fitted with three pairs of magnets allowing it to be attached to a tank, gun cupola, embrasure shutters, or pillbox doors. Early models had a 4.5-second delay, which sometimes did not allow time for the attacking soldier to seek cover. A 7.5-second delay fuse was introduced in May 1943. It could penetrate up to 140mm of armour and 51cm (20in.) of concrete. Three were allocated to each squad.

The 3kg tube charge (Rohrladung, Stahl, 3kg) was a bangalore torpedo 4.8cm (1.9in.) in diameter and 110cm (3.6ft) in length. The sections could be fitted together end-to-end to shove through barbed wire. A blunt nose cap was provided for the first charge.

Possibly the most feared weapon of the pioneers was the flame-thrower. The Flammenwerfer 35 had separate fuel and nitrogen cylinders. It could fire ten one-second bursts of Flammöl nr. 19 up to a distance of 3m. It weighed in at a backbreaking 36kg (79lb). The Flammenwerfer 40 was of the 'lifebuoy-type' with a donut-like fuel tank and a spherical compressed nitrogen tank in the centre. It weighed only 21kg (47lb) and retained the earlier model's range, but had a one-third reduction in fuel. The Flammenwerfer 41 had separate fuel and nitrogen cylinders and weighed 18kg (40lb). It only produced five flame bursts. The Flammenwerfer 42 was similar to the '41' but had an improved ignition system. When triggered, the '41' automatically ignited. It could not first 'wet down' the target with fuel, which could then be ignited by a flame burst. The '42' corrected this deficiency.

Standard demolition charges were incorporated into field-expedient anti-armour and anti-bunker charges, improvised hand grenades, booby traps, and 7 and 11kg (16 and 25lb) satchel charges. These charges were filled with TNT or picric acid and the first two covered with compressed paper, waxed paper, or Bakelite. The 1kg and larger charges had pressure-resistant zinc casings allowing them to be used underwater. The 100g boring cartridge (Bohrpatrone 28), 200g demolition container (Sprengkörper 28), 1kg (2.2lb) demolition petard (Sprengbüchse 24), and 3 and 10kg (6.6 and 22lb) concentrated charges (*Geballteladungen*) came with carrying handles allowing them to be used like satchel charges (see Plate E). To detonate these charges the blasting cap igniter set (*Sprengkapselzünder*) was issued. It consisted of a pull friction-igniter, one or two metres of time fuse, which could be cut to a shorter length, a Bakelite detonator holder, and a blasting cap (see Osprey Elite 100, *World War II Axis Booby Traps and Sabotage Devices*, Gordon Rottman, Osprey: Oxford, 2009).

BELIEF AND BELONGING

The perceptions of young German men were influenced by many factors. They were by no means universal or embraced to the same degree, but very widespread. Future soldiers were first influenced by their families. German family traditions were robust and close, providing German culture with one of its strong points. Uncles, aunts, and grandparents had much influence strengthening family bonds and reinforcing moral influences. The father was the head of the family without question, and by tradition was to assert a strong example. The mother too, the keeper of the home, was a symbol of strength. Parents were expected to take their family rearing responsibilities seriously and set an example. This was of course the 'ideal' German family. Not all attained this idyllic image, but it was prevalent.

NCOs and company officers were viewed as extensions of the German father figure; the company was the soldier's family and in many ways operated as such. Officers and NCOs sometimes referred to their men as *meine Kinder* (my children). Company officers and NCOs were expected to emulate the German concept of the strong father figure who looked out for the family's well being. In return the troops were expected to do their best following the example of their leaders. Squad leaders and other NCO leaders were expected to lead by example and care for their men.

The officers also led by example and regardless of the image portrayed by Hollywood most were not aristocratic, self-absorbed elitists, although those too existed. There was of course an image officers were expected to maintain. Regardless of the supposed classless Nazi society, the German officer corps resented 'commoners' entering its ranks with the army's expansion, as many new officers were former NCOs. Officers were expected to 'look like officers' and maintain a certain decorum and bearing. An officer may sometimes have

The origin of the flame-thrower

The story goes that prior to World War I during German manoeuvres, an unnamed major was ordered to defend his position at all costs. In danger of being overrun, and in desperation, the major picked up a fire hose and turned it on the attackers. During a staff critique he was asked what he thought he was doing. He replied he was spraying simulated burning oil on his attackers. This is said to have engendered the idea of the modern flame-thrower.

Such an event occurred in 1907 at Posen during a fortress assault exercise, but not exactly the way it is related. The Posen Fire Brigade was employed to spray water from a steam-powered fire pump to simulate liquid fire. This was done to demonstrate the possibilities of the flame-projector concept. A man-portable flame-projector had already been patented in 1901 by German scientist Richard Fiedler. The demonstration served to encourage further development. The first model was accepted in 1911 and two flame-thrower battalions were organized in 1914 under the command of a former Leipzig firefighter, Hauptmann (Captain) Hermann Reddemann. The first use of the *Flammenwerferapparate* (flame-projector apparatus) was against the French at Melancourt in the Verdun sector on 26 February, 1915. It was first used against the British on 30 July, 1915 at Hooge, Belgium.

Motorized and horse-drawn transport make their way over a temporary bridge with the assistance of pioneers. River and stream banks were often marshy and planking had to be laid on the approaches to bridge and ferry sites. (Nik Cornish at Stavka)

been referred to as a *Vomag*, a contraction of *Volksoffizier mit Arbeiter Gesicht*: a 'people's (meaning a common man) officer with a labourer's face'.

The new militarism of this time raised the soldier's profession to high levels, with it being an honour and privilege to serve the Führer and *Vaterland*. Soldiers were more important in status than the civilians they defended. To demonstrate this ideology, in the US Army the rank abbreviation 'p.f.c.' was said to mean 'praying for civilians'. This was in an army in which civilians were regarded as 'outranking' soldiers and p.f.c. was a desired 'rank'. In the German Army there was the fictitious rank of *Untergefreiter* (junior private). It referred to a civilian, lower than a private.

Regardless, the German soldier was taught that his highest duty was the defence of the fatherland, that he was protecting German culture from external threats and corruption. But, like it or not, he also swore to protect the Führer. Upon completion of basic training (US and Commonwealth soldiers took their oath upon joining the army) he swore a solemn oath to protect not the German constitution and nation, but the Führer himself through the Defence Force Oath of Loyalty to Adolf Hitler, 2 August, 1934:

Pioneers had a particularly difficult time in the high mountains where trees were nonexistent. Here, valuable poles are hauled upwards by mules. (Nik Cornish at Stavka)

Ich schwöre bei Gott diesen heiligen Eid, daß ich dem Führer des Deutschen Reiches und Volkes Adolf Hitler, dem Oberbefehlshaber der Wehrmacht, unbedingten Gehorsam leisten und als tapferer Soldat bereit sein will, jederzeit für diesen Eid mein Leben einzusetzen.

This can be translated as: 'I swear by God this sacred oath that I shall render unconditional obedience to Adolf Hitler, the Führer of the German Reich, supreme commander of the armed forces, and that I shall at all times be prepared, as a brave soldier, to give my life for this oath.'

German youths and young men were constantly barraged with propaganda. School teachers played an important role in their indoctrination. Of course there were many who did not agree, but nonetheless they were watched and encouraged to preach the party line. Movies, radio programs, magazines, books, pamphlets, and newspapers were important propaganda tools completely under party control. Discipline and political indoctrination were reinforced with symbols, paraphernalia, flags, banners, and music, both martial and patriotic. Among the HJ the uniforms, symbols, songs, rallies, torchlight parades, camaraderie, and bonding were indeed empowering to young boys hungry for Germany to regain its rightful glory and with their natural thirst for adventure.

In marshy areas and regions saturated by rain or snowmelt, corduroy roads (*Knüppeldamm*) were essential. They required huge numbers of trees and were labour intensive. In some areas logs had to be hauled in from great distances. (Nik Cornish at Stavka)

The popular motto '*ein Volk, ein Reich, ein Führer!*' – 'One people, one nation, one leader!' – expounded the concept of all German peoples unified as one nation under one supreme leader. There were many more mottoes reaching all segments of society: '*Mütters kämpf für eure Kinder!*' (Mothers, fight for your children!), '*Bilden sie Deutschland autark*' (Make Germany self-sufficient), '*Keiner soll hugern! Keiner soll frieren!*' (No one shall go hungry! No one shall be cold!), '*Arbeit, Treude, Zucht, Volkskameradschaft*' (Work, joy, discipline, camaraderie), '*Wir rüsten Lieb und Seele*' (We build body and soul), '*Durch Wehrwillen zur Wehrkraft*' (Through military will to military strength), are all examples.

Nazism and militarism permeated every aspect of society. Likewise, every aspect of the German Army uniform was chosen with care, signifying military traditions, its links to the past, and its backing by the Nazi Party. Even the double collar bars were noteworthy in that they were originally worn only by Guards units and signified the protection of the Crown. In the Heer, being worn by all units, they signified the protection of the State.

Kamerad – comrade, friend, comrade-in-arms – had a deeply serious meaning within the Wehrmacht forming a strong bond between men who fought together. This sprit of *Kameradschaft* (comradeship) was extended to *Frontkameraden* (front comrades), the fellowship of frontline soldiers (*Frontsoldaten*). The *Frontgemeinschaft* (front community) signified solidarity between *Frontkameraden*, amongst whom advancement was determined by proven skill, as bullets saw no distinction between ranks or classes. The *Frontgemeinschaft* philosophy was an outgrowth of the domestic *Volksgemeinschaft* (people's community), a spirit of social cooperation, unity, and duty to community and state fostered by the Nazis.

The realities of combat saw a change in the *Landser*, as it did with any soldier. After experiencing combat and with the seemingly endless war dragging on and on, the national socialist spirit diminished.

ON CAMPAIGN

The pioneers were given a wide variety of tasks in the field, many of which would not be found in their mission description. They aided the advance, delayed the enemy, built, demolished, rebuilt, and repaired. Many tasks required imagination and called upon their experience to accomplish. Besides serving as assault troops they were also employed as infantry later in the war when manpower was stretched. This was especially true when divisions had only six infantry battalions rather than the former nine and even entire battalions were lost. This was usually a secondary mission though as the services of the pioneers were still essential to the defence and maintenance of lines-of-communications.

The pioneer battalion

A divisional pioneer battalion (partly motorized) – *Divisions Pionier-Bataillon (Teile Motorisiert)* – was organic to infantry divisions. Other types of divisions' pioneer battalions, panzer and mountain for example, were somewhat differently structured and equipped. They bore the same number as their parent division – Pionier-Bataillon 12 der 12. Infanterie-Division. There were also non-divisional pioneer battalions attached to corps and armies with some collected together under *Pionier-Regiments-Stäbe*. There were also large numbers of specialized pioneer battalions such as bridge construction, landing [boat], fortress construction, obstacle, and construction battalions.

The 36-man battalion staff (*Bataillons-Stab*) consisted of the commander, a lieutenant-colonel or major, adjutant, special-duty officer, commissary officer, surgeon, assistant surgeon, and veterinarian along with staff NCOs and enlisted men. Alongside the staff was a 32-man signals platoon (*Nachrichten-Zug*) operating a few radios and the telephone system, the primary means of communication. Early in the war the battalion also possessed a 28-man band, the only battalion-size unit in the Heer to be authorized a band.

A heavy pontoon trailer is pulled by a 12-ton Sd.Kfz.8 heavy halftrack. Part of a bridge column's pontoon trailers would be towed by halftracks and the others by trucks. The halftracks were necessary to recover bridging equipment out of rivers and to tow other vehicles through riverside mud. (Nik Cornish at Stavka)

This group of *Pioniere* struggles to manoeuvre a small inflatable boat down a river bank. This photo demonstrates the type of uniforms and equipment carried late in the war. More and more frequently the *Pioniere* were employed as infantry to fill gaps in the overstretched front lines. (Pier Paolo Battistelli)

The 191-man 1st and 2nd Pioneer Companies (*1. und 2. Pionier-Kompanien*) had a company troop (*Kompanie-Trupp*), the headquarters, commanded by a captain. Included in the headquarters were the reporting NCO (equivalent to a first sergeant and also the company troop leader), a saddle master, gas defence and decontamination NCO, and two messengers with motorcycles, plus a light field car. There was also a 23-man company section (*Kompanie-Staffel*) divided into an ammunition and machine troop with three medium trucks and two trailer-mounted air compressors, a field kitchen train with a horse-drawn field wagon, horse-drawn field kitchen and two bicycles; a supply train with a medium truck and a field wagon, and a baggage train with a medium truck. The company train was often under-strength so the ill, lightly wounded, or injured were detailed to help out resulting in it being known as the *Troßkrank* (sick train).

PIONEER NCO

This pioneer *Unterfeldwebel* wears a uniform and equipment typical of the mid-war period (**1** and **2**). Prior to and early in the war only the company commander could grant permission to unbutton the tunic's top button on a hot day. Such formality disappeared during the war. A bread bag shoulder strap has been rigged as a means of breaking up the helmet silhouette and attaching camouflage. His equipment includes belt, support straps, two 30-round cartridge pouches, bread bag, water bottle with drinking cup, gasmask carrier with gas protection sheet strapped to it, and bayonet. He is armed with a Kar.98k carbine. He also carries special items issued to NCOs and officers: report/map case (*Meldekartentasche 35*), 6 × 30 universal binoculars (*Einheits-Doppelfernrohr*), march compass (*Marschkompaß*), field pocket lamp (*Felftaschen Lampe*), and army whistle (*Heer Pfeife*) (**3**) said to have a harsher sound than US and British whistles. Pioneer NCO shoulder straps (left to right) (**4**): *Unteroffizier, Unterfeldwebel, Feldwebel, Oberfeldwebel,* and *Stabsfeldwebel*. In the field the metal devices worn by *Feldwebel* and up were required to be removed for security reasons and lower rankers were to wear straps without embroidered devices. Pioneer hand tools issued to squads were the small wire-cutters (**5**), large wire-cutters (**6**), handsaw (**7**), pioneer spade with detachable handle (there was a similar pickaxe) (**8**), Glühzündapparat 37 exploder (**9**), and ignition tool kit (*Zünderwerkzeugtasche*) (**10**). Screening smoke was provided by the smoke hand grenade (*Nebelhandgranaten 39*) (**11**), smoke egg hand grenade (*Nebeleihandgranate 42*) (**12**), smoke fume cylinder (*Rauchröhr Nebel 39*) (**13**), and smoke candle (*Nebelkerzen 39*) (**14**).

There were three 52-man pioneer platoons (*1.–3. Pionierzug*) including a platoon troop (*Zug-Trupp*) with a 7.9mm Pz.B.39 anti-tank rifle, flame-thrower, and a one-horse field wagon. Its three 15-man pioneer squads (*Pioniergruppe*) were similar to a rifle squad, but larger, although in combat squads typically fielded eight to ten men. Each squad had an MG.34 machine gun. The anti-tank rifles were soon withdrawn to arm new infantry units. In 1943 the *Panzerfaust* appeared and a pioneer company was authorized 36 of these.

The third company would be motorized and similarly organized except that the unit had 198 men and was provided with 16 squad-carriers, one for each squad and platoon troop, and the rest were in the company troop and company trains section along with five medium trucks. The Heer suffered severe motorized transportation shortages and the 3rd Company would often lose its vehicles.

Pioneer companies each had 12 small (3m, three-man) and medium (5.5m, seven-man) inflatable boats (*Schlauchbooten*) for reconnaissance, troop and light equipment transport, and for making small pontoon bridges.

The light pioneer column (*Licht Pionier-Kolumn*) transported the battalion's ammunition reserve, demolition materials, barbed wire, sandbags, smoke candles and grenades, mines, commonly used power and hand tools, and minimal construction materials. The equipment included three air compressor trailers, 20 Dolmar gasoline two-man chainsaws, and six cutting torches. It was organized into a company troop of three platoons, each with three two-horse field wagons. The company-size unit also had a minimal equipment repair capability.

The pioneer battalion relied on manpower for work. There was no motorized construction equipment such as bulldozers, tractors, power shovels, dump trucks, cranes, or similar. Power saws were essential as local forests were the main source of construction materials. Another item seeing much use was the pneumatic hammer (*Preßlufthammer*). These were used for breaking up rock, concrete, and asphalt and drilling into the same to set demolition charges. There were also tamper heads for compacting road foundations and spade heads for digging through clay and soil.

A Pz.Kpfw. III tank is crossing a river on a Brückengerät B (bridging equipment B) pontoon bridge during the campaign in the West, May–June 1940. The Brückengerät B was the heavier bridging equipment of the time, and could carry up to 20 tons. Bridges could be constructed using adjustable steel supports in dry gullies and stream beds or where the water was too shallow for the pontoon floats. The traffic control paddle is white with a red centre. (Carlo Pecchi archive)

The 102-man bridge column B (Brückenkolonne B) was motorized. The six-man company troop had a light field car and three motorcycles. The 36-man *1. und 2. Ponton-Zug* had a light field car and a motorcycle in the platoon troop. The platoon had: eight 3.2m metal half-pontoons which could be fitted together end-to-end to form four full-pontoons, four bridge trestles, one ramp, four shore transoms, and four 16-ton crossing rails. To transport all of this were four eight-ton medium halftracks or heavy trucks with half-pontoon trailers, four medium trucks with half-pontoon trailers, two medium trucks with trestle trailers, and two medium trucks with shore transom trailers. The only differences between the platoons, besides the 1st being commanded by a lieutenant and the 2nd by an NCO, was that the 1st had a medium truck and trailer for a 7m motorboat (*Motorboot*) to aid in assembling the bridge while the 2nd had a trailer for six 6m storm boats (Sturmboot 39).

The eight-man *Ersatz-Zug* (replacement platoon) had a motorcycle with sidecar, two medium trucks with ramp trailers, and a medium truck with a trailer carrying ferry-liners. In the three trucks were carried 20 small and 24 medium inflatable boats, small bridge components, tools, and other equipment. The bridge column also had a 16-man supply and baggage train with one light truck, two motorcycles with sidecars, a fuel truck, and a truck-mounted field kitchen.

The two platoons together could assemble a 130m floating bridge supporting 4-ton loads, an 80m floating bridge for 8-ton loads, or a 50m 20-ton capacity bridge. The first two used half-pontoons and the 20-ton bridge required full pontoons. The pontoons could also be used to construct eight four-ton ferries, four eight-ton double ferries, two 16-ton ferries, or one 20-ton ferry. The bridge column was actually an equipment unit that transported and maintained the bridge equipment B (Brückengerät B), from which the pioneer companies constructed bridges and ferries, although the bridging troops assisted. These were removed from divisions in 1944.

LIFE IN THE FIELD

On campaign the pioneer was pushed to the limits of endurance. In addition to the fear, horrors, and dangers of combat, it was simply plain gruelling. There were endless road marches, much starting and stopping, delays, changes to orders and schedules (which more often than not made the unit late), and much 'hurry up and wait'. While all this was going on there was little news and information and what there was could often be confused by insistent rumours. Soldiers learned to cope and often tuned themselves out to what was going on around them. They focused only on their job and their platoon's mission. The weather could be counted on to be too hot or too cold, too dry or too wet. There were endless seas of mud or vast clouds of dust. Flies, gnats, and mosquitoes were often more than just annoying. There were no 'duty hours' or days off. It was endless work.

There was little or no warning of mission assignments and changes; they didn't know where they would spend the night, or when the next meal would arrive. Efforts were made to find shelter in

Members of the pioneer battalion's bridge column (a Pf.11 Pontonwagen for a 3.2m half-pontoon is in the background) brew coffee on a portable charcoal stove. Note the second man from the right wears a silver on dark green *Steuermann* (Steersman) badge over *Oberpionere* insignia indicating he is qualified to operate powerboats. (Courtesy of Concord Publications)

all but the fairest weather. Houses, barns, sheds, schools, warehouses, whatever could be found. There was no hesitation about turning out the occupants and taking over beds and food. Tents were seldom available. When forced to bivouac in the open, tents would be erected by buttoning together four, eight, or 16 shelter-quarters to house a like number of crowded men. In hard rains or high winds they were in for a very uncomfortable night. Since all the shelter-quarters were needed for the tent the ground was covered with pine or fir boughs, pine needles, leaves, or straw. This protected the troops from damp ground and mud, and insulated them from the chill as well as providing a degree of cushioning. There were no sleeping bags. Field bedding consisted of a greatcoat and one to three woollen blankets depending on the season. In extremely cold weather more blankets and quilts would be commandeered. In extreme cold as experienced in the Russian winter some form of shelter was essential.

Sleep was often impossible, as units kept moving through the night. There might be short halts in which some soldiers could nap an hour or so, but such irregular sleep was straining. Even when in a static position there was a constant need for sentries to guard the outer perimeter and also stand watch at each position. Patrols (*Frontbummel* – front strolls) might be sent out and there were always work details required just to keep the unit operational.

During what few breaks were available, if not sleeping or eating, the troops might simply talk, tell stories of home, repeat the latest rumours, play cards or chess, or simply sit lost in their own thoughts. Alcoholism was more of a problem than was recognized. Drunkenness on duty was a serious offense, but it frequently occurred, especially when local supplies were found in homes, shops, cafés, and restaurants. *Zielwasser*, literally 'target water', a 'hit the spot drink', was a common term for *Schnaps*, but also referred to any alcoholic beverage, the most common being *Kognak* (cognac), *Wein*, and vodka.

The Wehrmacht operated a number of radio stations throughout occupied Europe with programming specifically for soldiers. The *Soldatensender* broadcast popular music, news, talk shows, and propaganda. Especially popular were request concerts (*Wunschkonzert*) playing popular songs. Soldiers would also listen to foreign broadcasts. The BBC had a German service channel. The Ministry of Propaganda issued a directive, *Rundfunkverordnung*

Infantry and other units built their own bunkered quarters, although the logs and timbers may have been mass cut by the pioneers. (Nik Cornish at Stavka)

Pioneers put the finishing touches on a culvert-type bridge crossing a drainage ditch. Behind them is a captured Soviet Stdlinesh S-65 tractor, a very valuable prize for the pioneers. (Nik Cornish at Stavka)

(broadcasting order – shortened from *Verordnung über ausserodertliche Rundfunkmessnahmen* (decree concerning extraordinary broadcasting measures) making it illegal to listen to foreign radio broadcasts. A card was required to be posted on all radios reminding users that 'listening to foreign stations is a crime against the national security of our people'. The British operated several false radio stations broadcasting in German such as *Atlantiksender*, *Gustav Siegfried Eins*, and *Soldatensender West*. Germans tuning in to these channels would think they were official stations run by loyal, but discouraged soldiers talking about the disparity front soldiers suffered with senior officers and party officials living high and safe in the rear.

Field rations

Actually the proper term for food was field portions (*Feldportionen*); field rations (*Feldrationen*) were for horses. In the combat zone troops were issued provisions I (*Verpflegungssatz I*), a combination of fresh, preserved, and packaged foods. There were no equivalents to US C- and K-rations or British 24-hour ration packs.

The distribution of rations in combat was irregular at best, but the prescribed practice was to issue breakfast the afternoon or evening before. This was typically bread (enough for the entire next day), cheese (*Käse*), hard sausage (*Dauerwurst*), and marmalade or other preserves or butter. The sausage might not be available in which case another canned or preserved meat would be substituted or more cheese provided.

The *Feldkochunteroffizier* (field cook NCO) and his cooks would stoke up the *Feldküchenwagen* (field kitchen wagon) to provide hot coffee or tea for breakfast, which was distributed to platoons in insulated containers. Commonly known as the *Gulaschkanone* (goulash cannon) or *Futterkanone* (fodder cannon), it could be fired with wood, coal, or charcoal and towed with the fires burning. There were two versions, large and small, the former equipping pioneer companies. It could cook 175 litres (46 gallons) of stew, soup, vegetables, or boiled meat in its boiler kettle. There was also a 90-litre (34-gallon) coffee kettle. It was provided with six 12-litre insulated containers to transport food to frontline positions using a carrying harness.

Bread was essential to the *Landser*'s diet and came in several forms. *Kommißbrot* (commissariat bread) was a black rye bread, preserved with cinnamon and also known as *Karo Einfach* (simple square) or *Trockenes Brot* or *Dauerbrot* (dry bread) or *Stalintorte* (Stalin's pastry). *Kriegsbrot* (war bread) was palatable bread, packaged in cardboard cartons, intended to conserve ingredients and prolong its shelf life. It was made of 55 per cent rye flour, 25 per cent wheat flour, and 20 per cent potato meal, which delayed it becoming stale, plus shortening and sugar. With rye and wheat flour becoming scarce, barley, bean, buckwheat, Indian corn, oat, or pea meal were substituted. Crackers, described below, might be substituted for bread. The divisional bakery company baked fresh bread, but they could not always meet demand and distribution requirements. US army food-tasters stated that German rye breads were seldom to Americans' liking owing to the strong tastes and dryness.

The noon and evening meals were served hot if at all possible. Stew or soup was generally provided made with whatever meats and vegetables were available, typically potatoes, onions, turnips, beets, beans, and peas, the latter being known as *Wurmstichigen Erbsen* (wormy peas owing to 'visitors'). Sauerkraut was of course popular. Often mixed dried vegetables (*Gemüe*), packaged in cardboard cartons, tended to be hard and lumpy if insufficiently cooked after reconstituting with water, leading to them being called *Drahtverhau* (barbed-wire entanglement). Fresh meat was provided by the divisional butcher platoon when possible. Besides fresh meat, the platoon also provided sausage and soup bones. Supper was more of the same, but was usually a lighter meal than lunch or may have been similar to breakfast.

There were a wide range of other foods when available: canned sardines from Portugal and Norway, oranges from Spain and southern France, margarine in cans or toothpaste-like tubes, dried apples, chocolate and other candies, oatmeal, noodles, fruit conserve, and concentrated instant soup mix (*Wehrmacht-Suppekonserve*) issued to supplement iron rations or other lean meals.

Commonly consumed drinks included coffee and tea (both consumed hot and generally preferred with sugar), apple juice, and (generally disliked) reconstituted lemon juice. While real coffee was available from southern Europe, it was scarce. Chicory was grown in Europe and had long been blended with coffee to make *Kaffee-Ersatz* (substitute coffee). Chicory was popular

A Sturmboot 39 is run ashore. These assault boats were 20ft long and carried seven troops plus two crewmen. The 'mechanical oar', which protruded several feet aft of the boat gave it a speed of 15 knots and was also the means of steering. (Nik Cornish at Stavka)

prior to the turn of the century, but pure chicory 'coffee' was bitter and lacked caffeine and calories. Other substitutes (*Kaffee-Ersatz-Erstaz*) included roasted ground acorns/beechnuts, barley, chickpeas, and oats. There was also *Tee-ersatz* (substitute tea) made from strawberry leaves, *Braunstieligen* ferns, and many other plants. Without sugar these substitutes were extremely bitter. Other ersatz products included honey (*Honig-Ersatz*) and cocoa (*Kakao-Ersatz*).

Cans of meat large enough to feed two or three men included beef, pork, horsemeat, herring in tomato sauce and other fish plus corned beef hash (*Labkaus*), bologna-like *Schinkenwurst*, and spreadable liverwurst for bread and crackers. US Army food-tasters reported that most of the meats were of a good appearance and flavour, although they lacked salt. French- and Italian-made canned meat was also issued. The most notorious of these was Italian tinned beef known as *Alter Mann* (old man), *Asinus* or *Arsch Mussolini* (Mussolini's ass), or *Arme Mussolini* (poor Mussolini). The nickname is derived from the 'A.M.' stamped on the cans meaning Military Administration (*Amministrazione Militare*).

The *Marschportion* (march portion), the nickname for the *Marschverpflegung* (march provision), was intended to be eaten cold whilst in transit by foot, truck, or train. Provided in a paper sack or as separately wrapped items it consisted of one day's issue of bread/crackers, cold meat and/or sausage or cheese, bread spreads (marmalade or artificial honey), coffee/tea, and sugar.

A *Pionier* assault group ready for the attack. Note the large number of boxes and the variety of special carriers for engineer and other special tools worn by the soldiers, made either of leather or of canvas. The kneeling *Pionier* in the foreground is carrying on his back a leather signal cartridge pouch (on the left); there were two versions of this, the smaller for 12 rounds of 2.7cm, and the large one which could carry 18 rounds. (Private collection)

The iron ration (*Eiserne Portionen*) is often equated to the K-ration, but it was not a daily subsistence ration. It was only for emergency use, although there were times when it was all that was available. Two iron rations per man were carried in the company train and each man carried a half-iron ration (*Halb-eiserne Portionen*). A full ration had a 200g can of preserved meat (*Fleischkonserve*) of the same types as listed above, 150g of dried or preserved vegetables (*Gemüe*) or pea sausage (*Erbsenwurst*), 300g of crackers, 25g of substitute coffee, and 25g of salt (*Salz*). The half-ration consisted only of the canned meat and crackers. Only the company commander could authorize consumption of iron rations if regular rations could not be brought forward.

There were several types of crackers, biscuit, or hardtack. *Hartkeks* or *Panzerplatte* (armour plate) were six enriched hardtack crackers in a cellophane package and described as tasting like sweetened dog biscuits. *Zwieback* (twice-baked biscuits and nothing like the crispy thin baby teething crackers found in America) were thick crackers issued loose from tin or wooden boxes. Italian and French hardtack was also issued. *Duve Keks* were sweet crackers issued 18 to a paper carton.

EXPERIENCE IN BATTLE

It is impossible in a book this size to describe all of the types of combat actions a pioneer unit experienced. Their capabilities and missions were extremely diverse. A pioneer platoon might undertake greatly different missions in a single day, not knowing what would be in store next. Three example missions in different timeframes and areas by Pionier-Bataillon 12 der 12. Infanterie-Division are described here. It was destroyed in Russia and the survivors were rebuilt as 12. Volksgrenadier-Division in October 1944.

Bunkersturm, France, 1940

They had rolled into France under a storm of artillery fire, but it soon tapered off as the panzers far ahead closed in. The blitzkrieg had so far meant to the battalion only a great deal of manual labour. In Belgium they were mainly employed clearing wreckage, fallen trees, telephone poles, and hastily erected barricades from roads. They repaired a few incompletely damaged bridges and filled some shell holes. Mostly they marched, trying to keep pace with the infantry.

A flame-thrower assault group dashes through an artillery-blasted barbed-wire barrier; one man carries a Flammenwerfer 40. It was slightly lighter than the bulkier Flammenwerfer 35, but still offered the same range. (Pier Paolo Battistelli)

G

BUNKER ASSAULT, FRANCE, 1940

Described in detail in *Bunkersturm,* the pioneer squad and the rifle platoon it is supporting launch their attack on the French pillbox. The *Deckungstrupp* (covering troop) using the canal bank for cover have opened fire on the bunker with a flame-thrower and machine gun. Across the road the *Stosstrupp* (shock troop) is supported by the rest of the pioneer squad serving as the *Nebeltrupp* (smoke troop). The shock troop is contributing machine guns to the suppressive fire and the smoke troop is preparing to ignite smoke candles. Demolition men accompany the covering troop to move in from the other side of the bunker and attack the embrasures and door. From the rear, 7.5cm infantry guns and 8cm mortars commence their barrage on the woods to suppress the French company dug in there. The German concept was to keep the assault group small, make maximum use of existing cover and concealment reinforced by screening smoke, and employ maximum firepower to suppress the objective and adjacent covering positions and thus quickly overcome resistance and keep the attack's momentum rolling.

Issue smoke grenades and candles generated thick grey-white smoke. It contained zinc, making it dangerous to breathe for prolonged or frequent periods. It also displaced oxygen in an enclosed structure and could suffocate humans. The gasmask offered no protection, as it did not have an oxygen source. (Courtesy of Concord Publications)

In the afternoon they halted in a French village untouched by the passage of war. Word spread that they might remain here for the night. The company commander immediately ordered certain houses and shops with their overhead apartments secured for quartering, before any of the infantry came back. Men had already been scavenging for food and wine.

The *Unteroffizier* was feeling the comfort of the bed he expected to spend the night in when the *Zugführer* entered the apartment and spread a map on the table. Up ahead a French pillbox was blocking the road. A dug-in rifle company backed the position. Their *Pionierzug* was detailed to support the rifle company tasked with destroying the position. Each of their squads would be attached to a rifle platoon. The *Unteroffizier* would lead the squad attached to the platoon assaulting the pillbox. The troops were already collecting demolition materials and other equipment from the platoon's horse cart.

He left Gefreiter Fuchs (so nicknamed because of his red hair) to supervise assembling demolition changes as he went forward to the objective with the platoon leader and other squad leaders. They met the rifle company commander, were briefed on the situation and plan, and paired off with rifle platoon leaders.

From a grassy knoll he and the infantry *Leutnant* peered at the objective through their binoculars. The main asphalt road ran past them to their right and to the left was a parallel 20m-wide canal. Another road crossed the canal on a masonry bridge from the left and intersected the main road. Some 50m beyond the bridge was the French pillbox. It had two embrasures, the left-hand one for a machine gun and the right for a 25mm anti-tank gun. The pillbox, or bunker as the Germans thought of it, sat beside the main road separated by a ditch. The *Leutnant* said the bunker's entrance had a steel door on the side facing the road. The bunker covered the main road, intersection, and bridge. A barbed wire fence ran along the near side of the canal road from the bridge and along the main road's right side. The gap in the road was closed by some logs and hastily strung wire. It would not stop a panzer, but there were none here. It was in a good position and there was little cover on its approaches. About 100m behind the bunker was a wood line. An estimated two French platoons were dug in there covering approaches to the bunker from any direction. Another platoon was on the left side of the canal in a stand of trees covering that flank. The only way to approach the bunker was across the fields on the right flank, but the French in the woods covered that approach too.

The plan was for two rifle platoons to attack the woods through the brush and saplings with their pioneer squads providing screening smoke. Two regimental infantry guns and the battalion's mortars and heavy machine guns would lay a steady barrage on the woods. Once the infantry attack developed the mortars would shift to the French position on the other side of the canal (see Plate G).

A *Flammenwerfer* team attacks a concrete bunker reinforced with sandbags with a Flammenwerfer 35. It required a two-man crew to operate the flame-thrower. The operator's assistant turned on and off the fuel and pressure supply. Its range was 25–30m. (Pier Paolo Battistelli)

Gefreiter Fuchs brought the squad up with their equipment. The men were quietly excited, anticipating their first close-assault, but were apprehensive as well. Two were ready with the Flammerwerfer 35 and others were festooned with smoke grenades and candles. There were two 3m extended charges (*Gestreckteladung*) with over a dozen 200g charges wired to planks at 10–15cm (4–6in.) intervals. They would be pushed into the barbed wire as a substitute for bangalore torpedoes (*Rohrlandung*). Concentrated charges (*Geballteladung*) had been readied by wiring six stick grenade heads with detonators and handles removed around a complete central grenade. These would be placed against the door to blow it open or thrown into the anti-tank gun embrasure. A couple of double charges (*Doppelladung*) comprised of two 1kg demolition petards were fastened together with a short length of wire to be thrown over the gun barrel. With a short delay fuse they would sever the barrel. Two pole charges (*Stangenladung*) were also ready, 4m-long poles with 3kg charges wired to the ends. They were intended to be shoved into embrasures without the pioneer exposing himself to the field of fire.

The rifle platoon leader had read *Infanterie greift an* (*Infantry Attacks*) by Erwin Rommel, rumoured to now lead a panzer division. He adhered to the concept of keeping the shock troop (*Stosstrupp*) – the assault party – small and employing a large covering troop (*Deckungstrupp*) with at least two-thirds of the men. The small shock troop could more easily infiltrate and conceal itself to reduce casualties. Supporting the shock troop was the smoke troop (*Nebeltrupp*). The large covering troop placed suppressive fire on the target and could suppress adjacent positions.

The *Zugführer* spotted a blind area. The covering troop would crawl down the canal bank to the bridge. The bank was steep and brush covered, but it offered a concealed approach. It was out of range for the flame-thrower, but he hoped the flame-gunners could wade under the bridge and move within range.

The rifle platoon and pioneer squad broke up into the various troops and moved out. The *Unteroffizier* would lead the *Stosstrupp* with a rifle squad in support. The *Stosstrupp* crawled through the brush-covered field toward the bunker's side with its door. Part of the *Deckungstrupp* and the *Nebeltrupp* followed. Most of the *Deckungstrupp* crept along the canal bank. The company's other two platoons were moving in on the brush beyond the bunker.

A red smoke signal trailed into the sky and the 7.5cm infantry guns and 8cm mortars commenced their barrage on the woods. Things would happen quickly now. The *Stosstrupp* was near the edge of the brush facing the bunker's side. They would have to rely on every element being in the expected position as there were no direct communications. The *Deckungstrupp* at the bridge announced its presence by opening up with two machine guns firing directly into the embrasures with red tracers ricocheting about. Heavy machine guns were streaming tracers into the woods amid shell bursts.

The *Unteroffizier* could actually hear the flame-gunners at the canal. '*Fertig zum feuer!*' – Ready to fire! A yellow-orange flame jetted out from the canal bank on the other side of the bridge to engulf the bunker's front. A half-dozen bursts followed and then he heard, '*Letzter strahl*!' – Last burst! His best long-distance grenade throwers began chucking smoke grenades at the bunker. Others tossed heavier smoke candles just forward of their position. Before the *Stosstrupp* rushed the bunker they had to let the smoke screen develop to provide the necessary concealment.

A staged propaganda photo showing a *Pionier* tossing a stick grenade into the embrasure of a French bunker on the Maginot Line in 1940. The amount of equipment he is carrying, including the assault pack with explosive charges and *Pionier* spade, suggests how difficult it must have been to move carrying so much weight. (Pier Paolo Battistelli)

Two pioneers were ready to push two extended charges into the wire fence along the road. '*Fertig zum zünden*!' – Ready for ignition! The *Unterfeldwebel* yelled, '*All zusammen zünden*!' – All together, ignite! The pioneers ignited the fuses and called '*Brennt*!' – Burning! The explosion sent pieces of wire and posts flying. '*Hier Gasse*!' (Gap here!) shouted a pioneer, confirming the wire was breached.

The side door suddenly burst open and a man in khaki rushed out only to be cut down by a single machine-gun burst. The riflemen held their fire. The *Feldwebel* shouted '*Stosstrupp vorward*!' The demolition men ran forward at a crouch. Doctrine required squad and platoon leaders not to lead assaults themselves, but to direct from the rear. It would do no good if key leaders became casualties early in the assault. The *Feldwebel* was aware of high explosive and smoke mortar rounds landing on the French position on the other side of the canal.

The bunker's door had been shut. A cluster charge was thrown against the door and the assault pioneers piled into the roadside ditch. It detonated, but the door remained intact. A pioneer rapidly crawled across the ground on all fours dragging a pole charge. Staying outside the field of fire he ignited the delay fuse before jamming it into the larger embrasure and running like mad. It detonated, but the machine gun in the other embrasure kept firing. Their own machine guns maintained continuous fire.

Another pioneer darted forwards with a 7kg satchel charge and shoved it against the door. Running back he flopped like a rag doll to the ground. The charge detonated and another pioneer ran forward before the smoke and dust cleared. If the door had not been breached he would blow the door again. If it were open he would toss the charge inside. Inside it went and another detonation sent smoke bursting out of the embrasures.

Green smoke trails arched out of the far woods. The rest of the company was successful. The French position on the other side of the canal was quiet, the French probably having fled.

The infantry and pioneers assembled beside the bridge. Their losses were two dead and three wounded. No one has the stomach to search the smouldering bunker.

A boat landing-site built by pioneer troops. Such sites were used by couriers and boats to haul across small numbers of individuals. In the foreground is a 3m inflatable boat and at the small pier is a Sturmboot 39. (Nik Cornish at Stavka)

Ponton Brücken, Russia, 1941

They had stopped counting rivers and streams long ago. This was just one more to cross on the endless march eastward. The muddy road was littered with abandoned Russian equipment, overturned wagons, and dead horses. The *Unterfeldwebel* brought the platoon forward to find the situation chaotic. Elements of two infantry battalions were scattered about the river bend. Russian artillery was irregularly falling on both sides of the dung-coloured, 50m-wide river. Troops were frantically digging into the mud, NCOs and officers were running about trying to sort them out, and anti-tank and infantry guns were being rolled up and then left on the road as the crews sought cover.

While his men dug in the *Unterfeldwebel* found a battalion commander lying behind a fallen tree as staff soldiers dug slit trenches with mud flying. The *Bataillonführer* shouted the situation to him as more Russian shells sent gouts of mud skyward and fragments ripped bark from the tree trunk.

Two rifle companies had waded and swum across the river to establish a small bridgehead. He had to get more troops across before the Russians counterattacked in force. They had already fought off a probe. The Ivans had destroyed the timber bridge during their withdrawal. The pioneer platoon from the infantry regiment was preparing to cross to the far side and start digging an exit ramp in the steep bank. They needed to get a pontoon bridge across or at least set up a pontoon ferry to get anti-tank guns across. The pioneer battalion's bridge column was on the way. The *Unterfeldwebel* knew that; his platoon leader was back down the road awaiting it. His job was to prepare a launching site and select a covered site where the pontoons could be inflated.

A patrol crosses a river using a three-man, 3m small inflatable boat (klein Schlauchbooten 34). A pioneer company was equipped with 12 of these boats. They could be used to assemble floating infantry footbridges using a narrow plank walkway known as Bruckengerät C. (Pier Paolo Battistelli)

A column belonging to Panzergruppe Kleist is waiting to be ferried across a river on the Eastern Front, in the early stages of the campaign in 1941. Bridging equipment available to frontline units did not enable them to build bridges over large rivers like the ones encountered in the Soviet Union, therefore the only solution available was to use pontoon bridge sections to ferry vehicles, field guns, and equipment onto the other bank. Note in the foreground a 7m-long, shrapnel-riddled motorboat *(Motorboot)* used to erect pontoon bridges. (Carlo Pecchi archive)

He sent two squads to the shattered bridge to collect usable planks and timber. He led the other squad back to a gully a couple of hundred metres down the road. It was there that he found a company commander to order riflemen out of hiding. His men began hacking out brush with their spades and hatchets so the deflated pontoons could be laid out. Leaving them to guide in the pontoon platoon he trotted back to the launch site. He found two of his men staggering down the road to the aid station having been hit by shrapnel. A considerable quantity of lumber had been collected and they were scraping a ramp in the river bank. He found a very wet *weiss Pioniere* who reported that the far side shore was marshy and they needed planks to deck the exit ramp. They were collecting planks on their side, but needed more. The *Unterfeldwebel* would send over what he could spare. He then sent a detail to a battered log cabin to salvage logs. He asked for and received a rifle platoon to carry logs to the ramp. Seeing this work started he trotted back down the road. A truck had arrived with small inflatable boats and his squad was busy inflating four of them with foot-operated bellows. The *Zugführer* was angry because the promised air compressor had not arrived, and took his turn on the bellows.

The *Unterfeldwebel* hurried back up the road with most of the squad carrying two of the boats and passing walking wounded. Arriving at the launch site he found the artillery had lessened. Another rifle company was wading across, but bodies were scattered on the bank. They started lashing timbers to the 3m pontoons. Finding the infantry *Kompanieführer* he reported that they could ferry a 3.7cm anti-tank gun across when the other two pontoons arrived, if he could continue to use the loaned rifle platoon. With permission granted he sent part of the platoon to the gully to carry up the pontoons and help inflate the rest. The other men he set to tying lumber in bundles to float across to the far side.

The ramp was completed by the time the other two pontoons arrived. They completed the ferry, manhandled the gun aboard, and with the help of the gun crew, paddled across. They began building the deck for the next ferry and soon four more pontoons arrived. With them word came that the big 5.5m pontoons had turned up. The first ferry returned; its deck left bloodstained after the casualties were removed. It was not long before the two small ferries were shuttling guns, ammunition, and troops across and

A 3.7cm Pak.35/36 anti-tank gun is being loaded aboard a large rubber boat nicknamed a *grosse Floss Sack*. These pneumatic boats were 5.5m long, 1.85m wide and weighed 150kg. They could carry 1.5 tons, either an infantry group of 12 men plus one machine gun or the anti-tank gun with its crew. The boat crew included a helmsman and six paddlers – the passengers. (Private collection)

retuned with more casualties. Another four pontoons arrived and a third ferry was built. It made three trips and four more pontoons were brought up. They now had enough pontoons to start a bridge with a promise of four more. With the help of the *weiss Pionieren* they ran a pair of ropes across and started lashing the ferries to them. They had to remove some of the pontoons and rearrange them, and fit bridging planks between the ferries. Fortunately, the river was sluggish and required only minimal anchoring. The artillery fire was picking up though. More pontoons arrived and more were called for as shrapnel punctured three.

The first two 5.5m pontoons arrived, requiring a large number of men to struggle up the road with the bulky floats. It would require a long time to manually inflate enough medium pontoons to bridge the river so they began construction of another ferry. Work had no more than begun when a lucky artillery round blew it apart, killing and wounding over a dozen pioneers and infantrymen.

Even with pontoons partly deflated by shrapnel, infantry were streaming across the footbridge along with crews wheeling over anti-tank and infantry guns. Ammunition was being hauled across between rifle companies and then the wounded were carried across in the opposite direction. The *Unterfeldwebel* kept encouraging his men, pushing them, praising and cursing them as the moment demanded. The flow to the far side went on all night. Two 2¼-ton pontoon ferries were in operation and by dawn the rest of the pioneer company had arrived. They began construction of a bridge using the larger pontoons. The *Unterfeldwebel* and his exhausted platoon were sent to the rear for a well-deserved rest.

Two weeks passed. The *Unterfeldwebel* stood at attention before the *Bataillonführer* as he pinned the *Eisernes Kreuz 1.Klasse* (Iron Cross First Class) to his left breast pocket. The citation mentioned his efforts to bridge the river, but what it focused on was his labours to recover the pontoons and timber and move it all to the next crossing site after a replacement bridge had been built.

Straßesperre, Germany, 1944

The *Feldwebel* assembled his understrength platoon; 18 men were all they had left. They had lost almost as many to trench foot as to the enemy. Artillery fire could start bursting in the treetops at any moment or *Jabos* (fighter-bombers) might roar over with machine guns blazing. His *Pionieren* were cold, wet, exhausted, and most of all, hungry. A week earlier they had captured cases of American K-rations, but these were gone. Now all they received was a single, occasionally two, poor cold meals a day. Often this was *Frontkameradensuppe* (front comrades soup) of beans, potatoes, and ham – 'the comrades'. The concoction would keep well in cold/cool weather. In hot/warm weather vinegar was added to preserve it. It was often served in the morning and carried in the mess kit all day.

Their mission was to install mines, booby traps, and obstacles on a secondary road to delay the *Amis*. The infantry battalion, what there was of it, manning the front in this sector would withdraw down two forest trails leaving the primary and secondary roads free for the pioneers to emplace their dirty tricks. The *Amis* tended to ignore small trails. As previously experienced, the rear guard would probably withdraw early leaving the pioneers to hastily complete their task and make it out on their own (see Plate H).

The *Feldwebel* divided the platoon into three groups. Six men under Unteroffizier Fuchs were detailed to lay the two-dozen *Tellerminen* and eight *Schrapnellminen* just delivered. The *Feldwebel* would point out the sites where he wanted half of the mines installed. The rest would be emplaced around the roadblock (*Straßesperre*) that the bulk of the platoon would construct further to the rear. Unteroffizier Lehmann, his most experienced NCO, would head the three men detailed to emplace booby traps.

Three men were left at the site he had selected for the roadblock and with a scarce Dolman chainsaw they began felling trees. They had a hard time finding a litre of petrol for the chainsaw and would cut until they ran out or the saw died. The remaining men loaded up with mines and booby-trapping materials, leaving half at the roadblock. The heavy *T-Minen* cases, each containing four mines, were loaded into a wheelbarrow and a recently found baby carriage. The *Feldwebel* discussed mine and booby trap sites with the two *Unteroffizieren* as they moved down the road. Regardless of their exhaustion, the booby-trapping group was animated in their discussion of the traps they would use and where they would emplace them.

A *Bahnpionier* (railway pioneer) patrol setting up an MG.34 machine gun to face an enemy threat. Railway pioneers saw much use on the Eastern Front rebuilding Soviet railways, laying new rail lines, and repairing tracks after partisan or air attacks. Later they would have been used to destroy the railways to prevent their use by the advancing enemy. (Pier Paolo Battistelli)

These *Pioniere* are setting explosives to crater a road in Italy in 1944. In mountainous terrain, cratering roads was one of the more efficient ways to delay the advance of the Allied units. Note the use of artillery projectiles, in this case from a 15cm *schwere Feld Haubitze* (heavy field howitzer) round, used as a makeshift solution imposed by the lack of proper explosives. Detonating cord would be run from each buried projectile to explode them. (Private collection)

The road crossed a shallow stream and it was here they would emplace two of the T-mines. As the men uncased the mines and wired crossed metre-long sticks to their bottoms, two men removed their boots and trousers and scraped shallow holes in the icy stream bottom's mud. The mines were laid in the holes and armed. The sticks would prevent them from being pressed into the mud when a tank crossed, or from being washed away. Other men were digging holes for more mines. With the mines delivered other men went back to the roadblock to lay mines there. Pieces of pipe and tins were placed in some holes to distract *Ami* mine detectors. In fact only one mine was laid in the road, 30m from the ford. A wire was attached to the mine's carrying handle on the side and this attached to a pull-activated fuse fitted to a 200g TNT charge. The earth backfill was sloppy, making the mine easy to detect. The *Feldwebel* judged that the *Amis* would be looking for mines if one was detonated in the ford and would find them anyway. The anti-lifting charge might kill the man removing the mine. A messenger was sent forward warning the rear guard of the mined and booby-trapped road. Two mines were laid on either side of the road where trees were small enough for a tank to plough through as it avoided the road. These were well camouflaged and great care was taken laying leaves over them.

Some 100m back down the road two more T-mines were laid in water-filled ruts. One man walked over them making it look like only foot traffic had disturbed the mud. Two more were laid on either side of the road and well camouflaged, plus a couple of dummy mines of tins and pipe; there were no anti-lifting devices. The mines were planted different distances apart than the earlier ones to ensure a pattern could not be determined. About 20m to the side was an area of light brush offering good concealment. It was just the route cautious infantry would take. There Fuchs laid one of the S-mines, its tripwires hidden by the brush. If tripped, the mine would be fired about 2m high and detonate, showering the momentarily startled enemy with 360 ball bearings. Another 100m down the road a mine was planted on both shoulders, one with an anti-lifting charge. The *Feldwebel* was pleased Fuchs took the empty mine cases and arming clips with him so they would not alert the enemy.

The messenger sent to warn the rear guard caught up with them as they reached where the road passed through a wooden pole fence. The men showed the *Feldwebel* their handy work. Several fence poles, tree limbs, and planks were piled in the road gap and booby-trapped by three egg grenades with pull-activated fuses. One was obvious and two well hidden. Tankers would not burst through such a barrier, fearing mines, so infantrymen would clear it. A single mine was laid in the road 20 metres beyond the gap. Among the dead weeds and brush on their side of the fence two S-mines were planted with the tripwires running parallel to the fence, hopefully to be tripped by any enemy climbing over. One *Pionier* proudly showed him a field dressing packet apparently carelessly dropped. The *Amis* would often pick these up as they were short of medical supplies. A pull-wire had been threaded through the dressing's back and attached to a buried egg grenade. The leaves had been so carefully replaced it was impossible to tell that the ground had been disturbed.

At the roadblock the chainsaw had held up and over 20 trees had been dropped crisscrossed over the road and to the flanks, their limbs entwined. Men were wiring the trunks together, making it difficult to remove them. The booby-trapping group descended on the fallen trees emplacing pull-wired grenades, first tossing in scrap metal to confuse mine detectors. The remaining T-mines were planted in front of the felled trees where tanks might try and roll over them and on the flanks beyond the trees. The remaining S-mines were planted there too.

There was no way of telling how much damage their efforts would inflict, but it would provide a couple of hours for the rear guard to withdraw and for yet another defence line to be established further back in the Hürtgen Forest.

Behind the roadblock the *Feldwebel* found the company commander waiting beside a stack of machine-gun ammunition cans and *Panzerfausten*. He had a new mission for the platoon.

THE AFTERMATH OF BATTLE

Kampfgeist – battle spirit – represented absolute duty and obedience. Regardless of the corrupt Nazi cause many German soldiers performed their duty to the end. The *Feldwebel* and his diminished platoon dug *Panzergraben* (armour graves) – slit trenches providing them protection from over-running tanks – to cover their final roadblock. They could hear the progress of the *Ami* advance with the detonation of mines and booby-traps, but not as many as they had hoped. The experienced enemy was finding most of them. The lead tank was knocked out by a barrage of *Fausten* and burst into flames. It was a *Tommykocher* (Tommy cooker), as Shermans were known. The Americans merely pulled back and within minutes their *automatische Artillerie* responded with its *Feuerzauber* (magic fire) seeming never to miss.

The barrage survivors were ordered to withdraw before the next *Ami* attack. They carried the body of the *Feldwebel* with them. They had time to bury him and others. Their graves were marked by the standard *Birkenkreuz* (birch cross), the normal material used to make grave crosses and so called even if made of other wood. If possible a wooden device shaped like an Iron Cross was added with the casualty's name, rank, and dates of birth and death. Besides his *E-marke*, sometimes a beer or wine bottle with personal information on a scrap of paper was buried with him. His comrades might

The traditional *Birkenkreuz* (birch cross) used to mark the graves of so many German soldiers. (Courtesy of Concord Publications)

have sung '*Der gute Kamerad*' ('The good comrade'). This solemn song dates back to an 1809 poem, and was set to music in 1825. It equates to the American 'Taps' and 'The Last Post' of the British. It is sung to this day within the German armed forces. As with the national anthem, soldiers salute while the song is sung.

His family would print a 5 × 10cm (2 × 4in.) *Sterbebild* (death card) in his remembrance. Such cards displayed the uniformed soldier's photo, name, rank, (never his unit or place of death), date of death and age (seldom was the date of birth shown), something said of his character, and often a short poem or religious message. On the back might be a stock picture of a military grave, memorial, or religious scene.

Ich hatt' einen Kameraden,
Einen bessern findst du nit.
Die Trommel schlug zum Streite,
Er ging an meiner Seite
In gleichem Schritt und Tritt.

I once had a comrade,
You won't find a better one.
The drum was rolling for battle,
He was marching at my side
In the same pace and stride.

Eine Kugel kam geflogen:
Gilt's mir oder gilt sie dir?
Sie hat ihn weggerissen,
Er liegt zu meinen Füßen
Als wär's ein Stück von mir.

A bullet flew towards us
For him or meant for me?
It did tear him away,
He lies beneath my feet
Like it was a piece of me.

Will mir die Hand noch reichen,
Derweil ich eben lad'.
'Kann dir die Hand nicht geben,
Bleib du im ewigen Leben
Mein guter Kamerad!'

Wants to reach his hand to me,
While I reload my gun.
'Can't give you my hand for now,
You rest in eternal life
My good comrade!'

GLOSSARY

Ausbildungstaseln für der Pionier
Training Digest for Pioneers

Ausgabe für der Pionier
Issue for Pioneers (publication)

Bautruppen
construction troops

Birkenkreuz
'birch cross', slang for a soldier's grave cross

Bohrpatrone
boring cartridge

Brückengerät
bridge equipment

Deckungstrupp
covering group

Dienstzug
service uniform

Drillichrock
drill tunic

Drillichzug
drill uniform

Eihandgranate
egg hand grenade

Eisenbahntruppen
railroad troops

Eiserne Portionen
iron rations

Erkennungsmarke
identity tag

Feldausrüstung des Mannes
field equipment for enlisted men

Feldbluse
field tunic

Feldgrau
field grey (actually more green than grey)

Feldküchenwagen
field kitchen wagon

Feldmütze
field cap

Feldportionen
field rations

Feldzug
field uniform

Felftaschen Lampe
pocket lamp (torch or flashlight)

Feuerpause
ceasefire (also slang for a short break)

Flammenwerfer
flame-thrower

Frontzulage
front pay ('combat pay')

Geballte Ladungen
cluster charge

Gewehr
rifle

Grundausbildung
basic training

Haft-Hohlladunge
magnetic hollow charge

Heer
army

Hitlergruß
Hitler salute

Jabo
slang for Allied fighter-bomber

Kampf Rucksacken
battle rucksack

Kampfgeist
battle spirit

Kaserne
barracks

Klardraht
plain wire

Kugel-Ladung
ball charge

Landser
slang name for the German soldier

Lehrgang
training course

Mannschaften
enlisted men

Marschstiefel
marching boots ('jack boots')

Marschverpflegung
march rations

Minensuchgerät
mine detector

National-Sozialistische Deutsches Arbeiterparti – NSDAP
National Socialist German Worker's Party (Nazi Party)

Nebelhandgranaten
smoke hand grenade

Nebelkerzen
smoke candle

Nebeltrupp
smoke troop

Panzerfaust
'armour fist' anti-tank projector

Panzergraben
'armour grave' slit trench

Panzerknacker
  'armour-cracker' (nickname for *Haft-Hohlladunge*)

Pioneer-Bataillon
  pioneer battalion

Pioniergruppe/Pionierzug
  pioneer group (squad)/pioneer platoon

Pioniersturmgepäck
  pioneer assault pack

Pioniertruppen
  pioneer troops

Preßlufthammer
  pneumatic hammer

Rohrladung
  tube charge (bangalore torpedo)

Schlauchbooten
  inflatable boat

Schnuursteifel
  laced shoes

Schrapnellmine
  shrapnel mine

Schütze
  rifleman (private soldier)

Seitengewehr
  sidearm (bayonet)

Soldbuch
  pay book

Sprengbüchse
  demolition petard

Sprengkapselzünder
  blasting cap

Sprengkörper
  demolition container (charge)

Stacheldraht
  barbed wire

Stangenladung
  pole charge

Sterbebild
  death card (memorial card)

Stielhandgranate (**a.k.a.** *Kartoffelstampfer*)
  'potato masher' hand grenade

Stosstrupp
  assault troop

Straßensperre
  roadblock

Technische Truppen
  technical troops

Tellermine
  anti-tank mine

Tommykocher
  'Tommy cooker', slang for M4 Sherman tank

Truppenübungsplatz
troop training area

Unteroffizier-Anwärter
NCO aspirant

Urlaub
leave

Verbandpäckchen
wound dressing

Verpflegungssatz I
provisions I field ration

Waffenfarbe
branch of service colour

Wehrmacht
Defence Forces

Wehrmachtbeamten
Defence Forces official

Wehrsold
defence book

Zahlmeister
paymaster

Zünderwerkzeugtasche
demolition kit

BIBLIOGRAPHY

(Anon.) *Handbook on German Army Identification, 1943* (reprint)
(Toronto, no publication date)

(Anon.) *Handbook on German Military Forces, TM-E 30-451,* (1 March 1945)

Angolia, John R. and Schlicht, Adolf, *Uniforms and Traditions of the German Army 1933–1945, Vol. 3* (San Jose, CA, 1987)

Beiersdorf, Horst, *Bridgebuilding Equipment of the Wehrmacht 1939–1945* (West Chester, PA, 1998)

Buechner, Alex, *The German Infantry Handbook 1939–1945* (West Chester, PA, 1991)

Hauptmann, Zahn, *Pionier-Fibel* (Berlin, 1937)

Koch, Fred, *Flamethrowers of the German Army 1914–1945* (West Chester, PA, 1997)

Liere, Otl, *Pioniere im Kampf* (Berlin, 1940)

Mason, Chris, *Personal Effects of the German Soldier in World War II* (West Chester, PA, 2006)

Riebenstahl, Horst, D*eutsche Pioniere im Einsatz 1939–1945: Eine Chronik in Bildern* (Eggolsheim, 2001)

Zeska, Maj. von, *Das Buch vom Heer* (Berlin, 1940)

INDEX